I CAN GET IT FOR YOU WHOLESALE

I CAN GET IT
FOR YOU
WHOLESALE

A Musical Play

Book by
JEROME WEIDMAN
Based on his novel

Music and Lyrics by
HAROLD ROME

RANDOM HOUSE NEW YORK

FOR
Peggy and Florence

I CAN GET IT FOR YOU WHOLESALE *was first presented by David Merrick at the Sam S. Shubert Theatre, New York City, on March 22, 1962, with the following cast:*

(*In order of appearance*)

GIRL	Pat Turner
MISS MARMELSTEIN	Barbra Streisand
MAURICE PULVERMACHER	Jack Kruschen
MEYER BUSHKIN	Ken LeRoy
HARRY BOGEN	Elliott Gould
TOOTSIE MALTZ	James Hickman
RUTHIE RIVKIN	Marilyn Cooper
MRS. BOGEN	Lillian Roth
MARTHA MILLS	Sheree North
MARIO	William Reilly
MITZI	Barbara Monte
EDDIE	Edward Verso
BLANCHE BUSHKIN	Bambi Linn
TEDDY ASCH	Harold Lang
VELMA	Francine Bond
BUGGO	Kelly Brown
DELIVERY BOY	Eddie Verso
TRIMMER	Stanley Simmonds
GAIL	Wilma Curley
MISS SPRINGER	Pat Turner
LENNY	William Sumner
NORMAN	Stanley Simmonds
MANETTE	Luba Lisa
WESTERN UNION BOY	Eddie Verso
DELIVERY MAN	Don Grilley
ROSALINE	Marion Fels
NOODLE	Jack Murray

SAM .... Don Grilley
MOXIE .... Ed Collins
SHELDON BUSHKIN .... Steve Curry
EDITH .... Margaret Gathright

Directed by Arthur Laurents
Costumes by Theoni V. Aldredge
Settings and lighting by Will Steven Armstrong
Musical direction and vocal arrangements by Lehman Engel
Orchestration by Sid Ramin
Dance and incidental music arranged by Peter Howard
Production Supervisor Neil Hartley

SYNOPSIS OF SCENES

Time: 1937

ACT ONE

Scene 1: Seventh Avenue
Scene 2: Office of Maurice Pulvermacher, Inc.
Scene 3: Seventh Avenue
Scene 4: A Bronx Street
Scene 5: Mrs. Bogen's Kitchen in the Bronx
Scene 6: Club Rio Rhumba
Scene 7: Mrs. Bogen's Kitchen
Scene 8: A Bronx Stoop
Scene 9: Acme Modes, Inc.
Scene 10: Acme Modes Showroom

ACT TWO

Scene 1: Harry Bogen's Penthouse
Scene 2: Acme Modes, Inc.
Scene 3: Acme Modes, Inc.
Scene 4: The Club Rio Rhumba
Scene 5: Acme Modes Showroom
Scene 6: Mrs. Bogen's Kitchen
Scene 7: Office of Maurice Pulvermacher, Inc.

MUSICAL NUMBERS

ACT ONE

"Well Man" .... MISS MARMELSTEIN and MR. PULVERMACHER
"The Way Things Are" .... HARRY
"When Gemini Meets Capricorn" ...... RUTHIE and HARRY
"Momma, Momma" .... HARRY and MRS. BOGEN
"The Sound of Money" . . HARRY, MARTHA, MITZI, MARIO, EDDIE
"Family Way" .... MRS. BOGEN, HARRY, RUTHIE, TEDDY,
BLANCHE, MEYER
"Too Soon" .... MRS. BOGEN
"Who Knows?" .... RUTHIE
"Have I Told You Lately?" .... BLANCHE and MEYER
"Ballad of the Garment Trade" . . MISS MARMELSTEIN, RUTHIE,
BLANCHE, HARRY, TEDDY, MEYER and COMPANY

ACT TWO

"A Gift Today" ... SHELDON, HARRY, MRS. BOGEN, BLANCHE,
MEYER, RUTHIE AND COMPANY
"Miss Marmelstein" .... MISS MARMELSTEIN
Reprise: "The Sound of Money" .... HARRY
"A Funny Thing Happened" .... RUTHIE and HARRY
"What's In It For Me?" .... TEDDY and MARTHA
"What Are They Doing to Us Now?" .. MISS MARMELSTEIN,
BUGGO, TOOTSIE, MANETTE, GAIL, SPRINGER and CREDITORS
"Eat a Little Something" .... MRS. BOGEN and HARRY

ACT ONE

SCENE ONE

As the overture slowly fades, the curtain rises on a series of vignettes depicting New York City's garment center at the height of a busy day in 1937: grimy shipping clerks frozen in the act of shoving loaded hand carts along Seventh Avenue; pretty models displaying for buyers newly created fashions; operators bent over their sewing machines; cutters sending their whirling rotary blades slicing through stacked layers of silk; ragged apple venders hawking their wares on the sidewalk.

The music stops. The frozen figures come to life. Boys and girls, men and women, carrying placards appear among the workers. The placards read: "Please Help the Shipping Clerks of the Garment Center to Organize"; "Support Our Strike for a Decent Living Wage!"; "This Is America 1937?"; "Free Tom Mooney!"; "We Are Your Sons—Support Us!" The strike organizer, a GIRL *in a black leather jacket and a mannish felt hat, supervises the handing out of circulars. Some shipping clerks join the strike. Others are dubious. One reads and then flings away his circular. At once the* GIRL *in the black leather jacket gives the signal.*

GIRL   (*Shouts*) Get him!
        (*The striking shipping clerks turn on their reluctant comrade. His rack of dresses is hurled to the street. A fight starts. Everybody joins in. The fight turns into a parade of pickets as the set containing the office of* MAURICE PULVERMACHER *rolls in*)

3

Scene Two

Office of MAURICE PULVERMACHER. *The windows are marked in large letters, which the audience sees backwards:*

MAURICE PULVERMACHER, INC.
Gowns of Distinction
Street & Formal

MR. PULVERMACHER, *his back to the audience, is staring dejectedly out into Seventh Avenue.* MISS MARMELSTEIN, *his secretary, is holding a sheaf of papers: order forms, telegrams, etc. The telephone on the desk rings. She snatches it up angrily.*

MISS MARMELSTEIN   (*Shouts into phone*) Yes, yes! I told you ten times—later! (*She slams down phone and addresses* PULVERMACHER) I. Magnin says if we don't ship by tonight, we should cancel the order. So what should I wire back? (PULVERMACHER *merely shakes his head wearily. The phone rings.* MISS MARMELSTEIN *snatches it up*) Yes? Maurice Pulvermacher, Inc. Gowns of Distinction, street and formal. (*Covers mouthpiece, addresses* PULVERMACHER) What should I tell I. Magnin? (*Into phone*) Bahston? (*To* PULVERMACHER) Bawston! (*Into phone*) Filene's. Yes. Hello. I'm sorry. We don't know when we can ship your order. Look, it's the strike—it's the shipping clerks—yes, they've tied up the whole garment center. (*Covers mouthpiece and addresses* PULVERMACHER) You want to talk to them?

4

(*Enter* MEYER BUSHKIN. *He wears a cardigan. The lapels are stuck full of pins. A tape measure is draped around his neck*)

MEYER Mr. Pulvermacher, the goods for the Jordan Marsh order, it's laid out on the table. Should I cut?
(PULVERMACHER *shakes head, moves wearily to the desk and drops dejectedly into his chair*)

MISS MARMELSTEIN (*Irascibly*) Meyer Bushkin, for God's sake, what good does it do to cut dresses if we can't ship? (*Into the phone*) We'll ship, but on account of this strike we can't promise when—(*Her voice stops. She hangs up slowly*) They canceled. Should I call them back?

MEYER Mr. Pulvermacher, the Jordan Marsh order? Cut or not cut?

MISS MARMELSTEIN (*Warning him*) Bushkin! (*She takes a thermometer, shakes it down, thrusts it into Pulvermacher's mouth, and sings to* MEYER BUSHKIN "Well Man")
He's not a well man
And he's getting worse.
If he had any sense he'd be in bed
With a graduate nurse,

A couple big specialists,
High-priced consultations.
And outside, waiting in the hall,
Assorted large and small
Poor relations.

His aches have got aches.
His pains are in pain.
And what sizzles and frizzles inside there
All the smartest professors couldn't explain.

PULVERMACHER (*Removes the thermometer, stares worriedly at it, and sings:*)
They wouldn't know what.
Be quick as you can.
Time I haven't got,
You're dealing with not,
(*A few weak coughs*)
With not a well man.
(*The phone rings*)

MISS MARMELSTEIN (*Snatches up phone*) Yes? What? Well, wait a minute. (*Covers mouthpiece*) Mr. Pulvermacher, Harry Bogen is here to see you.

PULVERMACHER Who the hell is Harry Bogen?

MISS MARMELSTEIN One of our shipping clerks.

PULVERMACHER (*Furious*) Harry—*Judas*—Bogen!

MISS MARMELSTEIN He says he's got an idea that can help you.

PULVERMACHER (*Bitter*) Yeah. Into bankruptcy. He's the tall dark one?

MISS MARMELSTEIN (*She laughs*) Yes.

6

PULVERMACHER (*Shakes head*) They don't like him in the shipping room.

MISS MARMELSTEIN They're just jealous.

PULVERMACHER (*Turns*) Meyer?

MEYER He's smart.

MISS MARMELSTEIN He's very smart.

PULVERMACHER Too smart. And too much energy. Never trust people with too much energy.

MISS MARMELSTEIN *I* got energy

PULVERMACHER (*Angry*) Maybe I shouldn't trust you either.
(HARRY BOGEN *enters*)

MISS MARMELSTEIN (*Into phone*) Tell Mr. Bogen to come in.

PULVERMACHER (*To* HARRY) You don't wait to be asked.

HARRY You haven't got time, Mr. Pulvermacher.

PULVERMACHER (*Peremptory*) Meyer—

MEYER (*Pleading*) But, Mr. Pulvermacher.

MISS MARMELSTEIN (*Points to door*) Out!

PULVERMACHER Miss Marmelstein.

7

MISS MARMELSTEIN   (*Surprised*) Me?

PULVERMACHER   You.

MISS MARMELSTEIN   (*Points to door*) Out.
  (*She exits behind* MEYER BUSHKIN)

HARRY   (*Unctuous*) Mr. Pulvermacher, I want you to know
I am not here from the strikers. I'm here personally, to do
you a favor.

PULVERMACHER   (*Suspicious*) Why do you want to do me a
favor?

HARRY   You're my boss and I admire you, Mr. Pulvermacher.
You're one of the biggest manufacturers on Seventh Avenue, and you have a car with a chauffeur.

PULVERMACHER   (*Folding his arms*) So. Go ahead. Do me a
favor.

HARRY   O.K. When the strikers' committee comes here with
their terms, you tell them you won't hire them back—on
any terms. Tell them to go jump in the lake.

PULVERMACHER   (*Indignant*) What good will it do me with
them in the lake? I've got sixty thousand dollars' worth of
garments on the racks, I can't move them.

HARRY   *I'll* move them. I just organized my own company:
The Needle Trade's Delivery Service. My staff delivers the
stuff any place you want.
  (*He pulls a contract from his pocket*)

8

PULVERMACHER Where do you get a staff? Every shipping clerk is on strike.

HARRY If you tell them to go jump in the lake—no more strike. Those guys will be fighting to get work. I'll hire all I need.

PULVERMACHER (*Curious*) It doesn't bother you to break a strike?

HARRY Of course it bothers me. But what comes first? My own personal feelings? Or the favor I can do for a man like you? (*He drops into* PULVERMACHER'S *chair*) My service works out cheaper for you than a shipping clerk's salary. (*He waves the contract under* PULVERMACHER'S *nose*)

PULVERMACHER (*Lifts* HARRY *out of the chair and seats himself*) Tell me, young man. You think I can trust you?

HARRY All you have to do is pay me. How about it, Mr. Pulvermacher, yes or no?

PULVERMACHER (*Shakes head, turns away, and sings*)
I'm not a well man,
Get worse every year.
All the medical doctors give one look,
They're amazed I'm still here.

HARRY (*Reassuring*) You're a good-looking man.
(*Shows* PULVERMACHER *the contract*)

PULVERMACHER (*Turning away; sings*)
I should own a pharmacy

9

HARRY (*Hurrying around to the other side and again shoving the contract at* PULVERMACHER) My cousin has one.

PULVERMACHER (*Turning away; sings*)
    For just my prescriptions.
    My bills for only pills alone
    Would chill you to the bone
    With conniptions.

HARRY (*Hurrying around to the other side*) It must cost a fortune. However—

PULVERMACHER (*Turning away; sings*)
    What I have been through,
    No man could recite.
    It would make a heartbreaking play or story
    That only Turgenev, maybe, could write,
    A tragical plot.

HARRY It's a great contract.

PULVERMACHER
    So how can I plan

HARRY No fine print.
    (*He takes a fountain pen from his pocket*)

PULVERMACHER (*Sings*)
    You're dealing with not,
    (*A few weak coughs*)

HARRY Mr. Pulvermacher, this will save your business.

(*He thrusts the pen and contract into* PULVERMACHER'S *hands*)

PULVERMACHER   (*Sings*)
>   With not a well man.
(*He signs the contract*)

HARRY   (*Snatches back the contract and pen*) You'll never be sorry, Mr. Pulvermacher!

PULVERMACHER   (*Gathering all his strength, he bellows like Chaliapin to the world at large*)
>   *I'm not a well man!*
(HARRY *runs out. The office set moves off. We are back on Seventh Avenue. A shipping clerk named* TOOTSIE MALTZ *enters. He is pushing a handcart full of stacked strike signs*)

Scene Three

HARRY (*Comes running in and meets* TOOTSIE *at the center of the stage; waving the contract*) Tootsie, Tootsie, he signed!

TOOTSIE (*Awed*) You're kidding.

HARRY Look for yourself. I never thought I could get away with it. A lovely contract between Maurice Pulvermacher and us: The Needle Trade's Delivery Service.

TOOTSIE (*Examining the contract*) This is great, Harry.

HARRY (*Folding the contract*) Now all we got to do is to form the Needle Trade's Delivery Service.

TOOTSIE I borrowed *my* five hundred dollars. You got yours?

HARRY No—but I think I know where I can get it—I hope.

TOOTSIE (*Troubled*) Harry, you think we're doing the right thing? Breaking the strike?

HARRY (*Angry*) What the hell has right got to do with it? Look, I am fed up scratching and fighting for twelve-dollar-a-week jobs. Being ashamed to go home and see my mother —the way my father was. Being poor killed my father, but it ain't gonna kill me.

12

I CAN GET IT FOR YOU WHOLESALE

TOOTSIE (*Uneasy*) But, Harry, doing a thing like this—

HARRY (*Impatient*) Tootsie, look around. Who the hell do
they open the doors for? The guy with a fistful of money!
You think they care how he gets it? The only thing that
counts is that he's got it, and Tootsie—I'm gonna get it.
There are two kinds of people in this world—only two.
    (*He sings* "The Way Things Are" *as* TOOTSIE *exits,
    pushing the handcart*)

HARRY

    You're either a pitcher, dishing it out,
    Giving the orders, having the say,
    Or a catcher, waiting around to handle what
    The other feller sends your way.

    From now on, I'm telling you
    My catching days are through!
(*Chorus*)
You're the catcher, or the pitcher.
You're bamboozled, or you get richer.
You get done to or you do it.
That's the way things are!

    You're the loser, or the winner.
    You're the diner, or you're the dinner.
    You get screwed up or you screw it.
    That's the way things are!

    That's the way things are, and they've always been.
    If you're on the cold outside and you're wanting in,
    You gotta climb higher, always climb!

13

To hell with the rules!
Get used to the fools
Who have to be stepped on
From time to time!
That's the way
Things are.

Life's a cold-cash situation,
Bought and paid for—no obligation.
Never let your heart start bleeding,
Or your conscience itch.
You'll know you're succeeding
When you're called a son-of-a-bitch.
I'm a pitcher.
From now on I'm pitching.
I've caught on to the way things are!

Blackout

Scene Four

The lights come up on a Bronx Street. At left, a tenement stoop. People on way home from work cross in both directions. Among them is RUTHIE RIVKIN. *She carries a summer hat, purse, and folded evening newspaper. Harry enters as she reaches the center. He calls to her.*

HARRY Hi, Ruthie.

RUTHIE (*Turns and sees him*) Harry, for heaven's sakes, where'd you come from?

HARRY Other side of the Bronx. Mom and I are living on Honeywell Avenue now. How's your folks?

RUTHIE Just about the same—except a year older.

HARRY Holy smoke—been that long?

RUTHIE You moved away last March—the twenty-sixth.

HARRY You and your memory.

RUTHIE (*Shy*) Oh, well. There are some dates you just don't forget. (*Changing the subject abruptly*) I've got a job in a great big law firm downtown. Are you in law school yet?

HARRY No. I changed my mind about that.

RUTHIE I'm sorry.

HARRY I'm not. It takes too long and the money's too small. I see them downtown—men like Mr. Pulvermacher—making it big, smoking dollar cigars—and it drives me crazy. Who does everybody respect? The guy with a briefcase or the guy with a chauffeur? A big man has big money, Ruthie, and I'm gonna get it. Why are you smiling?

RUTHIE You're talking to me. It makes me happy.

HARRY You're about the only one I can talk to—even though you think I'm crazy.

RUTHIE No, I don't. I think you're marvelous. I think you can be anything you want to be.
  (*Her warmth upsets him. He turns to leave*)

HARRY Ruthie, you're too nice. I shouldn't have come up here.

RUTHIE I knew you were coming. (*He turns back*) On the subway, on my way home, I just happened to glance at the horoscope. Listen to this: "Capricorn—December twenty-second to January twentieth—Be prepared for a pleasant surprise in the form of a visit from an old school chum."

HARRY (*Cautious*) Say, that *is* funny. I better watch out for those things.

RUTHIE Oh, I read the horoscope every day. Let's see what it says about you. You're Gemini.

16

I CAN GET IT FOR YOU WHOLESALE

HARRY I am?

RUTHIE Of course. Gemini is May twenty-first to June twenty-first—and your birthday is May twenty-seventh.

HARRY You and your memory again.

RUTHIE Oh, well, there are some dates you just don't—(*Pause, then covers her embarassment by reading aloud in business-like fashion*) "Gemini. A good day to pay a visit to an old school chum who can be useful in helping you to get your new plan started." Harry, what plan?

HARRY Aah, you don't really believe in all that stuff.

RUTHIE Lots of people do.
(*They sing*: "When Gemini Meets Capricorn")

HARRY

Common sense says, "No,
It could not be so."

RUTHIE

But a great many folks keep track
Every single day
What astrologers say
Goes on in the zodiac.

HARRY

Common sense says, "No."

RUTHIE

Why be con or pro?
Keep an open mind, don't choose.

It's kind of fun to half believe it.
What's a person got to lose?
(*She moves to the stoop, sits down, and smiles as she pats the stone step beside her*)

HARRY

What's a person got to lose?
(*He sits beside her*)
When Gemini meets Capricorn
On her way from the I.R.T.,
Could be coincidence—

RUTHIE

Could be astrology.

When Capricorn meets Gemini
Right across from the grand concourse,

HARRY

Could be an accident—

RUTHIE

Could be some heavenly force.

BOTH

Did the planets plan it,
Or was it chance?
Hey, you stars over the Bronx,
Did you know the whole deal
In advance?

HARRY

Know all the while

I CAN GET IT FOR YOU WHOLESALE

RUTHIE

> How they both would smile,

BOTH

> How they both would stop,
> Feel their hearts go
> Clop—clop—clop.

RUTHIE

> When Capricorn met Gemini
> On a Hundred and Eighty-third,

HARRY

> Relishing every word they found to say.
> Could be the whole event was an accident—

RUTHIE

> Could be foretold in their horoscope
> Plain as day.

RUTHIE (*Reads the horoscope*) All right, Harry, "A good day to pay a visit to an old school chum who can be useful in helping you get your new plan started."
> (*He jumps up and strides away*)

HARRY Oh, it isn't really a plan—it's just a dopey idea, forget it.
> (*She gets up and follows him*)

RUTHIE Come on, Harry. Tell your old school chum. What plan?

HARRY Ruthie, I didn't have any plan when I came up here.

RUTHIE   But now—?

HARRY   (*All innocence*) Something just occurred to me, Ruthie. You *can* help your old school chum.

RUTHIE   (*Dry*) How much?
          (*They both laugh and sing*)

RUTHIE and HARRY
          Could be the whole event was an accident,
          Could be foretold in their horoscope
          Plain as day,
          Plain as day.
          (*He kisses her. She takes his face in her hands and kisses him. The lights go out*)

Scene Five

MRS. BOGEN's *kitchen in the Bronx.* MRS. BOGEN *is standing at the stove.* HARRY *comes in. He wears the sweater in which he appeared in previous scenes. He carries a hatbox, which he sets on table.*

HARRY   (*Excited*) Ma, I'm in business! I've got my own business!

MRS. BOGEN   I don't believe it.
        (*He runs to her and pulls out a sheet of paper*)

HARRY   Here, look! My own stationery! The Needle Trade's Delivery Service. H. Bogen, Pres.

MRS. BOGEN   (*Awed*) You're a president! How come?

HARRY   I finally had the guts. Oh, Ma, I'm so sure of myself, I can almost smell the money. Your little boy is gonna be somebody big.

MRS. BOGEN   Harry—

HARRY   Don't you believe in me?

MRS. BOGEN   Sure, but—

HARRY   But what?

MRS. BOGEN   Yesterday, twelve dollars a week, today a company. Harry, doesn't that take money?

HARRY   (*Airy wave*) Peanuts.

MRS. BOGEN   Where'd you get the peanuts?

HARRY   (*Crosses to the hatbox*) Ma, you understand business the way I understand cooking.
(*He pulls out a hat with flower trimming*)

MRS. BOGEN   What's this?

HARRY   A present.

MRS. BOGEN   What for?

HARRY   (*Kisses her*) If I'm happy, you gotta be happy.
(*He sings* "Momma, Momma" *as he puts hat on her head*)
What's the use of talking, it's as plain as plain,
Just from where I got my good sense and my brain,
All my better qualities, my looks and charm—
From a certain married lady that I love to pieces,
My mom!
(*He seizes her arm and dances her around the kitchen*)
Momma, momma, momma, momma,
Why did you have to be
Made so perfectly, mommaniu?

Momma, momma, momma, momma,
Who will I ever see
Half so good for me, mommaniu?

22

I CAN GET IT FOR YOU WHOLESALE

How could I ever meet
A girl as sweet
To make me care?
No matter what a honey,
No matter how much money,
Where's the one to compare
To my own

Momma, momma, momma, momma.
How can I help if I
Pass the other girls by, by, by!

Though I keep wide awake and looking for
A girl that I can take home and adore,
They just don't seem to make them any more
Like my own momma, momma, momma, momma, momma!
> (*The music continues as* HARRY *dashes out.* MRS. BOGEN
> *preens in front of a mirror.* HARRY *comes dashing back.*
> *He has discarded the sweater for a snappy suit. He car-*
> *ries a large dress box*)

HARRY   Ma, we did ten thousand last month!

MRS. BOGEN   (*At the sink*) That's wonderful.

HARRY   (*Dashed*) Aren't you impressed?

MRS. BOGEN   (*Shrugs as she wipes a dish*) Ten thousand is ten
less than twenty.

HARRY   (*Affecting an elegant accent*) Just give me time,
Mother dear, I'll get there. (*Sets down dress box, opens it,
pulls out a handsome robe which he drapes around her*

23

shoulders as he sings and dances her around the kitchen)
>Momma, momma, momma, momma,
>Why did you have to be
>Made so perfectly, mommaniu?

>Momma, momma, momma, momma,
>Who will I ever see
>Half so good for me, mommaniu?

(Music continues as he dashes out. She preens at mirror, then returns to sink. He comes dashing in again. Now he wears a homburg and a velvet-collared topcoat. He carries another dress box)

MRS. BOGEN *(At the sink)* How much you make this week?

HARRY *(Lofty)* Who has time to count?

MRS. BOGEN What have you got there?

HARRY *(Sets down the box)* A necktie. Listen, Ma. Tuesday, I want you to cook up the best dinner you ever made.

MRS. BOGEN How do you know you're gonna be hungry Tuesday?

HARRY It's for a guy named Teddy Asch. He's the best sales-man on Seventh Avenue. And Meyer Bushkin and his wife.

MRS. BOGEN Harry—what are you up to?

HARRY I'm getting out of the delivery business and starting my own dress business. Aren't you proud?

24

I CAN GET IT FOR YOU WHOLESALE

MRS. BOGEN Harry!

HARRY All I gotta do is get Teddy Asch and Meyer Bushkin to come in with me—and put in ten thousand dollars each.

MRS. BOGEN What are you gonna put in?

HARRY Ten thousand dollars.

MRS. BOGEN That's nice. Where are you gonna get it?
(*He gives her a long stare, then prances away and, as he sings, opens the box, pulls out a silver-fox scarf and drapes it around her*)

HARRY (*Sings*)
Momma, momma, momma, momma, dy-didda-dy-dee-dee!
Here, slip into this, mommaniu.

MRS. BOGEN
Right now in the middle of the blintzes?

HARRY
Bang with a one two three!

MRS. BOGEN
Harry, what has got into you?

HARRY
So try it on for me.
I gotta see
Is it your size.
Oh, dear, it's much too baggy.
Down here in front it's saggy.

MRS. BOGEN

Don't be smart, mister wise guy!
So let it be baggy, saggy,
My neck it couldn't choke.
It's enough to just look and stroke.

HARRY

Down in the park they'll faint when you go by.

MRS. BOGEN

A real live silver fox for me, oh my!
When my friend Ethel sees it, oh, she'll die!

HARRY

Momma, momma, momma, momma, momma!
(*They dance*)

HARRY

Momma, momma, momma, momma,
How can I help if I
Pass the others girls by, by, by?

Though I keep awake and looking for
A girl that I can take home and adore,
They just don't seem to make them any more
Like my own

MRS. BOGEN and HARRY

Momma, (Harry), Momma, (Harry), Momma, (Harry),
Momma, (Harry), Momma, (Harry), Momma, (Harry),
Momma!

Blackout

Scene Six

*The Club Rio Rhumba. The bartender (*MARIO*), cigarette girl (*MITZI*), and* EDDIE, *a waiter, are at the left at the bar. They are idly rolling dice. Down the steps at the right comes* MARTHA MILLS, *a blonde, showgirl. She trips on step, but does not fall.*

MARTHA   Damn it!

MARIO   Well, well, if it isn't the lady herself.

MARTHA   Hi, Mario.

MITZI   Thanks for the tickets, Miss Mills.

EDDIE   We loved you in the show.

MARIO   Wish you did more.

MARTHA   (*Sits on a stool at the bar*) So do I. Listen, I'm meeting a Mr. Bogen.

MARIO   He's in the men's room.

MARTHA   (*Gets up*) Well, me for the ladies' room.

MARIO   Shall I buzz you when he comes out?

MARTHA   (*Dry*) Don't you always?

27

MARIO   Cheer up. You'll be a great star next season.

MARTHA   How many seasons have you been saying that, Mario?
  (*She disappears into the ladies' room. At once the door of the men's room opens and* HARRY *steps out*).

HARRY   (*Eager*) She here yet?

MARIO   In the powder room.

HARRY   (*Anxious*) You didn't tell her I was here?

MARIO   Oh, no, Mr. Bogen.

HARRY   (*Sits at the bar*) And don't forget about the telephone.
  (MARIO *waits.* HARRY *gives him a dollar*)

MARIO   (*Smiling*) No, sir, Mr. Bogen, I won't.
  (MARTHA *comes out and sits at bar.* MARIO *serves drinks and exits*)

MARTHA   I suppose I should say I'm sorry to be late, Mr. Bogen.

HARRY   (*Smiles*) I don't like girls who show up on time for a first date. Means they're anxious.

MARTHA   Well, most men would consider that flattering.

HARRY   Everybody has his own way of getting flattered.

MARTHA   And what's yours, Mr. Bogen?

HARRY   I like to get what's hard to get. Call me Harry.

MARTHA   (*Cool*) I will—when you get it.
  (*Enter* EDDIE, *carrying a telephone*)

EDDIE   Call for you, Mr. Bogen, sir.

HARRY   Not now. I'm busy.

EDDIE   The gentleman said it's urgent, sir.

HARRY   I don't care how urgent it is. I don't want to be interrupted.

EDDIE   Yes, sir, Mr. Bogen.
  (*He exits with the telephone*)

MARTHA   (*Cool*) Did you have to tip Mario a lot to arrange that little scene?
  (HARRY *reacts, then grins*)

HARRY   Ten bucks

MARTHA   Five would have been enough.

HARRY   It was.
  (*She reacts, then grins*)

MARTHA   Harry Bogen. Yeah.

HARRY   Yeah.

MARTHA   You know, when you came backstage last night, I thought you were just a little boy—looking for an autograph.

HARRY   You make dates often with little boys who collect autographs?

MARTHA   Only when they look like they might grow up into big boys who can hand out autographs on big fat checks. (TOOTSIE *enters down the steps*)

TOOTSIE   Harry, excuse me . . .

HARRY   Oh, hi, Tootsie. (*Pats vacant stool at bar*) Put it there.

TOOTSIE   I—uh—didn't mean to—uh—interrupt—but I got your message to come over.

HARRY   Well, whether you meant to or not, you have. So sit down. (*He turns*) Martha, this is my partner, Tootsie Maltz.

MARTHA   Tootsie? Is that a family name?

TOOTSIE   Well, actually . . .

HARRY   Tootsie, this is Miss Mills. Martha Mills. She sings in that great big Broadway hit, *Smile Out Loud*.

TOOTSIE   Harry's told me a lot about you, Miss Mills.

MARTHA   (*Dry*) He must have talked all day. He just met me last night.

TOOTSIE   (*Hastily*) Oh, I didn't mean—

MARTHA   (*Dry*) I know *you* didn't.

30

TOOTSIE (*Starts to leave*) Harry—maybe—I mean, whatever it is you wanted to see me about—maybe some other time?

MARTHA (*Rising*) I'll just go put on a new face.

HARRY (*Restraining her*) I like the one you're wearing. Stick around. This won't take long. (*He turns as she slips back up on the bar stool*) Tootsie, how do you like this delivery business of ours?

TOOTSIE How do I like it? Harry, what kind of a question is that?

HARRY We're partners. Suppose you didn't like it? How do you suppose that would make me feel?

TOOTSIE Harry, what's the matter with you?

HARRY I don't know, Tootsie. Neither do the doctors.

TOOTSIE Doctors?

HARRY They want me to go away for a year. Maybe two. Complete rest. That's why I asked you to come over tonight. The business. It's all yours, Tootsie. You can buy me out.

TOOTSIE Harry, buy you out? With what?

HARRY You've saved eighty-seven hundred bucks out of the business, haven't you?

TOOTSIE You don't mean to tell me you're willing to sell out your half for a lousy eighty-seven hundred bucks?

HARRY Okay, make it ten thousand.

TOOTSIE But I only got eighty-seven hundred.

HARRY I'll take your note for the balance.

TOOTSIE Thanks.

HARRY It's a deal. Now, here's a check made out to me for
eighty-seven hundred dollars. Sign on the dotted line. That's
it.
(TOOTSIE *signs*)

TOOTSIE Gee, Harry. Thanks a lot.
(HARRY *hustles* TOOTSIE *to the stairs*)

HARRY Now, you meet me in Golig's office tomorrow morning at ten-thirty and we'll finalize the details and draw up
a note. So long, Toots. Thanks for coming.

MARTHA (*Raising her glass*) Bye, Tootsie baby. (TOOTSIE
exits) I don't know much about the delivery business—
but my guess is that this one is worth a lot less than eighty-
seven hundred clams.

HARRY In two weeks it won't be worth a fish.

MARTHA And what will you be worth?

HARRY Look, when we made this date last night, why didn't
you ask me to bring along my rating from Dun and Brad-
street?

MARTHA (*Laughs*) I forgot. Mr. Bogen, I'm a simple, honest
girl. I don't have a sick mother to support, I haven't got an

old grandmother who depends on me. I've just got me. And a certain number of years in which to arrange my future.

HARRY   I'm a simple, honest guy who would like to help you with those arrangements.

MARTHA   Don't you have any other obligations?

HARRY   Me, I'm completely alone in the world.

MARTHA   Well, you could start by doing something about my wrists, Mr. Bogen. They get awfully chilly.

HARRY   Would a diamond bracelet do the trick?

MARTHA   For one wrist—if it were wide enough.

HARRY   It'll be wide enough.

MARTHA   (*Laughs*) Oh, I've got a feeling—

HARRY   I got the same feeling—

MARTHA   Yeah.

HARRY   Yeah.
   (*They dance and sing* "The Sound of Money")

MARTHA

There's every indication
We two should get together.
We're tuned to the same station,
Birds of a feather.

HARRY

I feel a strange attraction.
We share the same reaction,
Antennas both aware
Of that certain something calling,
Calling to us in the air!

The sound of money,
The lovely sound of money!
I find it quite appealing,
A feeling you may share.

It seems to cheer me,
Whenever it is near me.
It elevates my spirit
To hear it in the air.

What savage splendor,
That mating call of legal tender,
As dollars meet in sweet surrender.
And when the romance ends, dividends!
(*The bartender, cigarette girl, and waiter enter. They join in the dance*)
The sound of money,
Enchanting sound of money!
Here's hoping I keep saying
My whole life long,
"Dear, they're playing our song,"
The sound of money.
(**HARRY** *sings the following counter-melody while the others softly sing the chorus*)

I CAN GET IT FOR YOU WHOLESALE

A chauffeur standing by
Makes me hear angels harmonize.
A penthouse in the sky
Whispers lullabies.

A great big yacht about to dock
Makes such a couth and soothing sound.
A block of blue-chip stock—
Music all around.

What savage splendor
That mating call of legal tender
As dollars meet in sweet surrender
And when the romance mounts
Bank Accounts!

Riding in a Bentley
Or a Rolls, the clock tick-tocks
Much more sentiment'ly
Than a tune of Offenbach's.

"Dear, they're playing our song,"

MARTHA

Listen!

ALL

The sound of money.
(*The dance comes to a climax with* HARRY *waving a
fistful of money, which the others frantically reach for*)
Blackout

Scene Seven

MRS. BOGEN's *kitchen in the Bronx. Evening.* MRS. BOGEN, RUTHIE RIVKIN, *and* BLANCHE BUSHKIN *are tidying up after a meal.*

BLANCHE   (*Holds up a dish she has just dried with a kitchen towel*) Where does this go?

RUTHIE   On there, Mrs. Bushkin.
    (*She points to a sideboard*)

MRS. BOGEN   (*At the sink*) For Ruthie to help with the dishes, all right. By us Ruthie is like family. But you—you're a guest, Mrs. Bushkin.

BLANCHE (*Peering off into the living room*) To me it looks like any minute now me and my Meyer we'll be part of the family too.

MRS. BOGEN   They're still talking?

RUTHIE   (*Also peers into the living room*) Well, Harry is still talking.

MRS. BOGEN   Mr. Asch and Mr. Bushkin?

BLANCHE   Still listening. (*She comes back from the living-room door*) If you only knew, Mrs. Bogen, how worried I

36

was until tonight. The ten thousand dollars for the new dress business—Meyer and I saved it for the children's college tuition. But I'm not worried any more. Now I've seen Mr. Bogen's—I mean Harry—now I've seen his family—what could go wrong? A mother who cooks so well, and a nice steady girl he's going to marry like Miss Rivkin here.

MRS. BOGEN   It's Ruthie—please.

BLANCHE   I mean Ruthie.

MRS. BOGEN   (*Cautious*) You said Harry mentioned something to you about marrying?

BLANCHE   To me, no, not exactly. But from the way he said to Meyer—you know how men, when they're alone together, you know how they talk.

RUTHIE   (*Embarrassed*) Now, really.

BLANCHE   (*Laughing*) It's all right, it's all right, from Big Mouth Blanche you didn't hear a word.

HARRY   (*Entering from the living room*) Ladies, meet Seventh Avenue's newest and hottest manufacturer of forty-nine ninety-fives, Acme Modes, Inc. (*Gestures toward the living-room door. Enter Meyer Bushkin*) Our factory man and top designer, Meyer Bushkin. And, and, our sales genius, Teddy Asch.

   (*Enter* TEDDY ASCH. BLANCHE *is hugging* MEYER. MRS. BOGEN *is hugging* HARRY. TEDDY *is alone*)

RUTHIE   (*Goes to* TEDDY) Congratulations.

TEDDY   I hope they're justified.

HARRY   (*Laugh*) Did you ever see such an optimist?

TEDDY   I've been on Seventh Avenue a long time.

HARRY   So has Meyer—which is why I wanted both of you.

TEDDY   (*Dry*) And our ten thousand apiece.

MEYER   Oh, Teddy—the three of us are going to make a wonderful team.

HARRY   (*To* MEYER) He knows it. (*To* TEDDY) Now come on, won't you?

TEDDY   Well, like I told you: I was bitten once before and it's kind of hard to forget. But—yeah, I think we have a good chance.

HARRY   Let's drink to Acme. Ma, we're going to drink to Acme.

MRS. BOGEN   A toast.
(*She goes to the sideboard for a decanter*)

TEDDY   Look, I gotta make with the feet. Thanks a lot, Mrs. Bogen. To be honest with you, I don't know what swung me over—your son's gift of gab, or your cooking. I haven't eaten food like that since my own mother, she should rest in peace, passed away.

MRS. BOGEN   Have a little wine, Mr. Asch.

HARRY   What's with the Mister? He's in the family now. Ma, meet Teddy.

38

I CAN GET IT FOR YOU WHOLESALE

MRS. BOGEN   (*Smiles*) How do you do, Teddichkeh?

TEDDY   (*Surprised*) That's what my own mother used to call
me.

MRS. BOGEN   What else?
(*She kisses* TEDDY. *He embraces her. Music starts. They
dance and sing* "Family Way")

MRS. BOGEN
Teddichkeh meet Ruthaleh.
Ruthaleh meet Teddichkeh.

RUTHIE and TEDDY
Pleased to meet you, $\begin{cases} \text{Ruthaleh.} \\ \text{Teddichkeh.} \end{cases}$

MRS. BOGEN
Dye, dye, diga, diga, dye!

ALL
Dye, dye, dye!

RUTHIE
Teddichkeh meet Meyeraleh.
Meyeraleh meet Teddichkeh.

TEDDY and MEYER
Pleased to meet you, $\begin{cases} \text{Teddichkeh.} \\ \text{Meyeraleh.} \end{cases}$

RUTHIE
Dye, dye, diga, diga, dye!

ALL
Dye, dye, dye!

HARRY

Ev'ry one meet Idaleh,
A mamaleh of mine.
What can it hurt, Idaleh,
A glass Passover wine!
Teddichkeh meet Blancheleh.
Blancheleh meet Teddichkeh.

BLANCHE and TEDDY

Pleased to meet you, $\begin{cases} \text{Teddichkeh.} \\ \text{Blancheleh.} \end{cases}$

ALL

Charmed to make the acquaint-
ance!
Dye, dye, diga, diga, dye!

TEDDY   (*All excited*)

Dye, dye!

> (MRS. BOGEN *has been pouring wine for all the guests.*
> BLANCHE *is already getting giggly on the mere smell of
> the wine.* TEDDY *is really getting into the spirit of the
> thing. He joins in the introductions and in urging on
> the dancing. Those who aren't being introduced sing
> the counter-melody*)

ALL

Teddichkeh meet Idaleh.
Idaleh meet Teddichkeh.

Pleased to meet you, $\begin{cases} \text{Idaleh.} \\ \text{Teddichkeh.} \end{cases}$

Dye, dye, diga, diga, dye.
Dye, dye, dye!

Blancheleh meet Ruthaleh.
Ruthaleh meet Haraleh.

(*Counter-melody*)

Hye, diga, dye, dye, dye.
Hye, digga, digga, day.
Hye, diga, dye, dye, dye.

Hooray, the family way!

Hye, diga, dye, dye, dye.
Hye, digga, digga, day.

40

I CAN GET IT FOR YOU WHOLESALE

Pleased to meet you, {Ruthalah.
Blancheleh.
Haraleh.

Hye, dye, diga, diga, dye!
Dye, dye,

Hye, diga, dye, dye, dye,

Hooray, the family way.

TEDDY

Oh, I feel so—I don't know.
I can't find words to say.
Looka me—who thought I'd be
In the family way!

Hye, diga, dye, dye
Dye, dye—hey!
Dye, dye—hey!
Dye, dye! Dye, dye!

BLANCHE   (*Giggling*) Ooh, what he said!
    (*As everybody sings,* RUTHIE, *flushed and carried away,
    becomes the leader of the group. She starts the counter-
    melody while the others softly sing the first two melo-
    dies and gradually join her*)

Oh, what a pleasure to be
Part of one family,
Not alone with no one to care for
    you!

Live one for all, all for one,
Give and get lots of fun,
Have a home with love blooming
    there for you!

MRS. BOGEN

Come shine, come rain!
You've got who to share
The laughs and the pain.

MEYER
Plural is best any day.
Singular is passé:

ALL
I say hooray for the family way!
> (*The number develops into a grand kazatske with everyone dancing and singing.* TEDDY *is bubbling over with a new-found good fellowship.* BLANCHE *is a little tipsy.* MEYER *is trying to join in and still keep an eye on* BLANCHE. MRS. BOGEN *is dancing as though she were at her own wedding.* RUTHIE *is somehow the central spirit of all the gaiety.* HARRY *is happily joining in. The number comes to a climax of music, dance and laughter. It finishes with everybody breathless and elated*)

Hooray the family way!

MEYER   Blanche, the baby.

BLANCHE   (*To* MRS. BOGEN) Good night.

HARRY   Come on, family, I'll get you a taxi! It's on me!
> (*He hustles out* BLANCHE *and* MEYER)

TEDDY   (*To* MRS. BOGEN) I gotta make with the feet. I'm late for El Morocco.

MRS. BOGEN   Good night, Teddichkeh.

RUTHIE   Good night, Teddy.

TEDDY   Good night.
> (*He exits*)

42

MRS. BOGEN (*Puts her arm around Ruthie*) So—here we are—all of a sudden two big business ladies.

RUTHIE It's exciting, isn't it?

MRS. BOGEN Who ever thought the day would come we'd look out the window—(*Gestures to the window*) and like in the movies—we'd see big chimney stacks belching smoke, and over the whole thing a big sign: "Harry Bogen Enterprises!" (*Quiet*) All from my cooking, and your five hundred dollars.

RUTHIE (*Quick*) How did you know?

MRS. BOGEN Harry and I have always been very close.

RUTHIE Well, I was certainly glad to do it for an old friend.

MRS. BOGEN And he did pay it right back? Didn't he?

RUTHIE Well—he wanted to. But I wanted to invest in Acme Modes. I insisted. I believe in Harry, Mrs. Bogen, and he needs that.

MRS. BOGEN Ruthie, what can I say—take care.
 (*Sings* "Too Soon")
  Too soon, don't give your heart away.
  Too soon, oh no, don't let it go.
  Too late, you'll learn,
  If you're not loved in return,
  The world's a hundred times more lonely.

Wait, wait awhile.
True love won't run away.
Love that's for real will stay.
You may have tears tomorrow,
If too soon you give your heart today!

RUTHIE (*Indignant*) Honestly, Mrs. Bogen, the way you talk about your own son—I sometimes think—

MRS. BOGEN (*Quiet*) I think, too. Not only sometimes. All day. All night. Because he *is* my son.

RUTHIE There's nothing wrong with being ambitious. Harry wants to get ahead. He wants to make a success.

MRS. BOGEN (*Sings*)
Making a success is like baking a cake.
Just from out of the thin air you never make.
Eggs and flour, milk and sugar you must use—yes?
The same likewise with success.

I can see on the label, how it would read.
Success contained herein is made from the finest ingredients,
Five hundred borrowed dollars, one Bronx brain, very clever,
Lots of nerve, pure ambition, and assorted people.
Only the best people, we guarantee
Are being used in this time-tested recipe.

MRS. BOGEN Ruthie, take care. Don't run. Walk.

RUTHIE You don't get very far—walking.

44

MRS. BOGEN

> Too soon, don't give your heart away.
> Too soon, oh no, don't let it go.
> Too late, you'll learn
> If you're not loved in return,
> The world's a hundred times more lonely.

> Wait, wait awhile!
> True love won't run away.
> Love that's for real will stay.
> You'll maybe cry tomorrow,
> If too soon you give your heart away.
> (*The music continues*)

RUTHIE You sound like—like you don't trust Harry.
(HARRY *re-enters. He stops short and looks sharply at the two women. The music continues softly*)

HARRY (*Cheery*) Well, Ma, you and your cooking sure carried the day.

MRS. BOGEN (*Quiet*) Me and my cooking—and Ruthie.

HARRY What's Ruthie got to do with it?

MRS. BOGEN If Macy's sells more than Gimbel's, the window trimmings they have nothing to do with it?

HARRY Are you implying that I invited Ruthie here tonight just to create an impression on my new partners that I'm a respectable man with a nice respectable girl?

45

MRS. BOGEN The implying you can leave downtown. Up here in the Bronx we talk plain English.

HARRY In plain English, I invited Ruthie here tonight because—

MRS. BOGEN Yes, Harry?

HARRY Because I'm taking her out. Good night, Ma.

MRS. BOGEN (*As he leads* RUTHIE *out*) Ruthie. (RUTHIE *and* HARRY *stop at the door*) You're a nice girl.
>   (*They exit.* MRS. BOGEN, *alone on stage, watches them go, sighs, starts washing the dishes, and sings*)
>> Wait, wait awhile!
>> True love won't run away.
>> Love that's for real will stay.
>> You may have tears tomorrow
>> If too soon you give your heart today.
>> *Blackout*

Scene Eight

The stoop in front of RUTHIE's *house. Midnight.* HARRY *and* RUTHIE *come in. She is carrying a souvenir doll. They walk politely, not very close, and stop in front of the stoop.*
The orchestra is playing "When Gemini Meets Capricorn."

RUTHIE Well, thank you. I had a most enjoyable evening.

HARRY Me, too. I've never been to the Lewisohn Stadium before. I never realized all that—you know—all that music—could be so enjoyable. I mean, thanks very much for widening my horizon.

RUTHIE Me, too. I mean thanks very much for taking me to that place—where you bought me the doll—

HARRY The Hottentot Club.

RUTHIE Yeah. Thank you very much, I really mean it. I've never been to a night club before.

HARRY (*Surprised*) You're kidding.

RUTHIE No, it's true.

HARRY I thought you went out all the time.

47

RUTHIE Oh, I do. That's the beauty of living in New York.
I go out all the time.

HARRY What sort of guys you go out with?

RUTHIE Oh, no sort of "guys," really.

HARRY You mean, alone?

RUTHIE Well—yes, frankly. Mostly alone. (*She sits on stoop
and sings* "Who Knows." *He sits beside her*)
New York is a wonderful town, a very stimulating place to be.
It's full of galleries and exhibitions, most are absolutely free.
And concerts like at Lewisohn Stadium, plus at Carnegie Hall.
We sit way up top, but it's wonderful acoustics.
That's where it sounds best of all.

Art lectures at the Metropolitan. I attended ancient Greece the
other day.

HARRY Really?

RUTHIE (*Nods*)
The modern dance and ballet at the Y.M. and W.H.A.
And legitimate plays on Broadway. Don't you think Odets is
great?

HARRY Great.

RUTHIE
Not downstairs, of course. We get last-minute balcony down
at Gray's Cut Rate.

I CAN GET IT FOR YOU WHOLESALE

What better way can a single girl with leisure spare time find,
Than to go around, broaden out her background, also improve
    her mind?
Plus it gives more chance for meeting up with people,
    wouldn't you say,
Such as certain members of the opposite sex she hopes to get
    involved with some day.
And who can tell, who knows when they might come one's
    way!
      (*She rises and moves forward*)

Who knows when I'll see him, who knows?
Or why it will be him, who knows?
Perfect he doesn't have to be,
Good looking, or rich, and smart,
Long as he's crazy after me,
And we see heart to heart.
      (*He rises and comes up beside her*)
Who knows when he'll be there, who knows?
One day he'll see me there and hold out his arms.
First he'll kiss me, say he loves me, and then propose!
But why, where, when, who knows?
      (*The music continues.* HARRY *is moving closer to* RUTHIE,
      and then seems to stop himself)

HARRY

    Well, I guess like Teddy Asch would say,
    I'd better make with the feet.
    Tomorrow's gonna be a real busy day
    Before the new deal is complete.

Good night.
> (*He moves off*)

RUTHIE   Good night. Harry . . . (*He stops*) that nice Mrs. Bushkin and her husband . . .

HARRY   Yeah, they're great.

RUTHIE   Yeah, well, she said they put money in your business.

HARRY   Ten thousand dollars.

RUTHIE   I've got ten, Harry. (*He reacts*) Well, Papa has, but it's for me, or rather for the man I marry.

HARRY   (*Smiles*) You shouldn't go around telling that to guys in joints like the Y.M. and W.H.A.

RUTHIE   I've never told anyone till today.

HARRY   So why me?

RUTHIE   Ever since P. S. 12 I've had a dream.

HARRY   A dream?

RUTHIE   About you. That some day you'd be a great big important lawyer. Maybe even a Supreme Court judge. Why not?

HARRY   (*Angry*) Great big important lawyer, yeah! College, four years. Law school, four years. On what? Hey, what is this all of a sudden? Are you making me a business proposition or something?

RUTHIE   Sure. I'm tired of being respectable Ruthie. I'm going to try being practical Ruthie. So it's a business proposition. What do I do now?

HARRY   (*Hard*) Wait for the other guy to say yes or no. (RUTHIE *turns away. He melts. He sounds helpless*) Ruthie, it's not you, it's the Bronx. You want to stay, I got to get out. I can do it on Meyer's ten thousand. What you're entitled to get for your ten, I haven't got to give.

(HARRY *exits.* RUTHIE *goes to the stoop, picks up her doll and sits. She sings*)
One day he'll see me there and hold out his arms.
First he'll kiss me, say he loves me and then propose.
But why, where, when . . .
(*She stuffs the doll into her mouth to still her sobs, as the orchestra finishes the song. The lights fade*)

Scene Nine

ACME MODES, INC. The factory area is at the left rear. VELMA, *a shopgirl, enters, calling as she crosses hurriedly.*

VELMA   Miss Marmelstein, Mr. Bushkin wants more buttons for twenty-two-o-two!

BUGGO   (*Shouts as he enters*) Miss Marmelstein!

DELIVERY BOY   (*Entering with a basket of flowers*) They want someone to sign.

BUGGO   (*Takes the basket as Miss Marmelstein enters and signs the receipt. He reads the card aloud*) Hey, Sam, get a load of this: "Dear, they're playing our song—I hope. Happy Opening." Signed: "Martha Mills."

VELMA   (*Re-enters hurriedly, shouting*) Mr. Bushkin! We're outa green velvet buttons for seven-o-four!

TRIMMER   (*Enters, harassed*) Miss Marmelstein! I don't get another trimmer to help, I'll never be finished by four o'clock!

PRESSER   (*Entering behind* GAIL, *a model*) Oh, Gail, take off eight-o-eight, I'll press the hem.
        (*The model steps out of the dress*)

GAIL (*As she exits*) The shoulder straps, too.

VELMA (*Hurrying across*) Now they want *pink* buttons!

MANETTE (*Enters with a torn shoulder strap*) Where's that damn baster?
    (MEYER BUSHKIN *enters*)

MEYER I'll fix it. I'll fix it. (*He works on* MANETTE's *shoulder strap as he calls:*) Buggo. Go down bring up corn-beef, pastrami sandwiches for everybody!

BUGGO On the house?

MEYER Why not?

ALL Hooray.

MEYER Who has time to go out to lunch today?

MEYER How about malteds?

BUGGO Malteds?

MEYER What else?

MANETTE Would you make mine an egg cream?

MEYER And halvah for dessert. Miss Marmelstein, the whole thing out of petty cash.

MISS MARMELSTEIN (*Annoyed*) This kind of cash is petty?

53

MANETTE   Come on, tightwad!

MISS MARMELSTEIN   All right, when Mr. Asch comes in here screaming, I'll tell him to go talk to you.

MANETTE   Any time, honey. That Mr. Asch sure is cute.

GAIL   I'll take Harry any day.

MANETTE   So change your name to Martha.
(HARRY *enters as everyone except* MISS MARMELSTEIN *exits*)

HARRY   Miss Marmelstein! Miss Marmelstein. Everything okay?

MISS MARMELSTEIN   (*Ticking off the items on her pad*) I think so. Liquor, appetizers, sandwiches, decorations.

HARRY   (*Snaps fingers*) Bourbon for Miss Springer. The Bon Ton Shops in twelve major cities. That's all she drinks, you know. And she never eats. But boy, when she buys—*if* she buys—you're in! And—oh, yes. Send a check for this right away
(*Hands her a bill, which she scans*)

MISS MARMELSTEIN   (*Puzzled*) One diamond bracelet? What does Acme Modes want a diamond bracelet for?

HARRY   (*Tweaks her cheek*) It's a publicity gimmick. But nobody's to know except you and me. So draw the check, right away.
(MISS MARMELSTEIN *laughs and exits.* MANETTE *enters*)

54

MANETTE This what you mean, Mr. Bogen?

HARRY No, dear. (*He takes a flower from the side of her dress and places it down the front of her dress. She giggles*) And get Mr. Bushkin to fix it so it keeps on tickling.
    (*He slaps her on the rear and* MANETTE *exits as* MRS. BOGEN *enters*)

MRS. BOGEN You have to pay them, too?

HARRY (*Laughs and sings*) Momma, Momma, Momma, Momma. Whatcha doing here so early? I told you come four o'clock.

MRS. BOGEN (*Dry*) If I come when you tell me, I'll only see what you show me.

HARRY (*Pulls out a small package*) Well, early birds gotta get rewarded.

MRS. BOGEN (*She opens the package. It contains a jeweled locket. She is delighted*) A picture of Papa.

HARRY (*Turns the locket over*) And Mama.

MRS. BOGEN (*Sighing*) If only Papa were alive to see this.

HARRY If Papa were alive—

MRS. BOGEN All right. So he talked too much. But you'd be better off with more of him and less of me.

HARRY Wrong. When you're around, I'm the best.

MRS. BOGEN   Maybe I ought to be around more.

HARRY   What are you trying to say, Ma?

MRS. BOGEN   (*Points to herself*) Oh, Harry, the suit, the fur, the locket—it all costs money

HARRY   So?

MRS. BOGEN   Where'd it come from? You haven't even opened your doors yet—now, don't tell me to stick to my cooking.

HARRY   Well, you should. I'm so sure about Acme, I'll bet you tomorrow morning everybody on Seventh Avenue—from Mr. Pulvermacher up and down—they'll be taking off their hats to me.

MRS. BOGEN   Why?

HARRY   Because I'll be rich.

MRS. BOGEN   Is that a reason? Oh, I made a stop on my way here.
   (*She turns as Ruthie enters*)

RUTHIE   I told your mother this was a bad idea, but I wanted to see the dresses.

HARRY   (*Pauses, then shouts*) Miss Marmelstein!
   (DELIVERY BOY *enters with a basket of flowers*)

Barbra Streisand, Elliott Gould, Marilyn Cooper, and
Lillian Roth, as MISS MARMELSTEIN, HARRY BOGEN,
RUTHIE RIVKIN, and MRS. BOGEN

DELIVERY BOY   Where do these go?

HARRY   Out front. (MISS MARMELSTEIN *enters as the* BOY *exits with the flowers*) Miss Marmelstein, get the Tyson Ticket Office. Talk to Eddie. I want two down in front tonight for the Metropolitan Opera House, and I don't care if he has to buy them back from Otto Kahn.

MISS MARMELSTEIN   Yes, Mr. Bogen.
(*She exits*)

HARRY   Oooh, those stone seats at that Lewisohn Stadium. Tonight we're sitting soft. Come on out back. I'll give you an advance look at the line.
(HARRY, RUTHIE *and* MRS. BOGEN *exit and* VELMA *enters*)

VELMA   (*Harassed, as she crosses and exits*) Mr. Bushkin, now we're out of pink velvet buttons for nine-o-nine.
(TEDDY *enters carrying a batch of papers*)

TEDDY   Miss Marmelstein! Miss Marmelstein! (WESTERN UNION BOY *enters with a batch of telegrams*) What the hell do you want?

WESTERN UNION BOY   Sign, please.
(MISS MARMELSTEIN *enters as* TEDDY *signs the* BOY's *receipt*)

MISS MARMELSTEIN   Oh, you got the mail. Good.
(*She takes batch of papers from* TEDDY *as the* BOY *exits*)

TEDDY   Damn right I got it. How else am I gonna find out

57

what goes on around here? (*Waves a sheet of paper under her nose*) What's this for?

MISS MARMELSTEIN   Perfume.

TEDDY   Eight hundred seventy-two dollars' worth?

MISS MARMELSTEIN   You can't get everything wholesale.

TEDDY   Very funny. I wanna know what in God's name we're doing with eight hundred seventy-two bucks' worth of perfume?

MISS MARMELSTEIN   It's presents. For the buyers.
    (HARRY *enters*)

TEDDY   Whose bright idea was that?

HARRY   Mine.

TEDDY   (*Turns*) It ain't enough you're shoveling caviar into them like it was mashed potatoes? You gotta also give them a bath in Chanel Number 5? I want you to listen to me, bright boy.
    (DELIVERY BOY *enters with case of champagne*)

DELIVERY BOY   Where's this go?

TEDDY   (*Points left*) Out!

HARRY   (*Points right*) Out front! I been listening to you—
    (*He and* TEDDY *move toward each other, fists clenched. As*

58

DELIVERY BOY *exits with champagne,* MEYER *enters just in time to separate* HARRY *and* TEDDY. HARRY, *furious, continues his speech*) for nine weeks—ever since we signed our lease —and everything I heard, you put it together with a nickel, it'll get you in the subway.

MEYER   Harry, please, not now!

HARRY   (*To* MISS MARMELSTEIN) Draw the check! I'll sign it!

TEDDY   (*To* MEYER) For this you took your ten thousand bucks out of the savings bank?
(*Another* DELIVERY MAN *enters with a large wreath marked "Success." He carries it across the stage and exits*)

MEYER   (*Troubled*) Harry—

HARRY   (*Tough*) Meyer, comes four o'clock and those models walk out on the platform—you just see to it they're wearing that line. I'll take care of everything else.
(*Enter* BLANCHE, *unobserved. She listens*)

TEDDY   (*Sarcastic*) Sure he will. Including your kid's college tuition.

MEYER   Harry—maybe what Teddy says we should listen to?

HARRY   Teddy's a salesman like you're a designer. Let him stick to his job the way you stick to yours, and stay out of the front office the way you stay out. You don't understand money and Teddy's afraid of it—which is why neither of you will ever be anything more than you are now—good at your jobs. But me, I'm very friendly with money. We're developing a romance. That's why I was the one to start this firm. That's why I'm the one to run it. I'm gonna keep running it—my way. So what Teddy says won't change nothing.

(*He stalks out*)

TEDDY (*Shouts after him*) That's right—it won't!

MEYER What's this craziness about money?

TEDDY He's in love with it. When you're in love you think you can do anything.

MEYER Teddy, what can we do?

TEDDY Nothing—it's too late. He's peed away every nickel we started with. We got nothing in reserve. At four o'clock—when we roll those dice—if it comes up snake eyes, we're down the drain.

(TEDDY *exits.* BLANCHE *comes up and touches* MEYER. *He turns*)

MEYER Blanche!

BLANCHE Meyer, I hope you don't mind my coming early? I just couldn't wait. It's all so wonderful! My Meyer, a tycoon!

MEYER Blanche, it's all up in the air. Nothing is settled yet. You heard what Teddy said.

BLANCHE I also heard what Harry said. Personally, I'm not worried. Harry is the one I'm listening to. Meyer, I don't want you to be worried either.

60

I CAN GET IT FOR YOU WHOLESALE

MEYER You know what I'm really worried about? You.
These last few weeks, working so hard, night and day, I'm
at home like a boarder. A whole week I haven't seen you.

BLANCHE Of course you have. In the morning when I bring
you coffee, and at night when I bring you the bicarbonate.
(MEYER *sings* "Have I Told You Lately?")
Sometimes suddenly, it comes over me—
How you love me!
Often through the day,
As I work away

I'm impatient so—just to let you know
How I'm likewise.
And I resolve to get home early
With roses for my girlie,
And kiss her hand, her lips, her nose, and say:

Have I told you lately
You look so lovely,
Each time I see you, my heart melts away?

In the rush of little every-day things,
Sometimes you don't say things
You mean to say.

Have I mentioned lately
I'm glad you took me,
Instead of hooking someone with a million or two?

When I think of all the girls I could have been stuck with,
I sure was in luck with
The one I drew.

Have I told you lately
How much your husband loves you?
> (*The music continues as they dance*)

MEYER   Blanche, have I told you lately?

BLANCHE   What?

MEYER   You look so lovely.

BLANCHE   (*Fluffing out the skirt of her dress*) Acme original.

MEYER
In the rush of little every day things
Sometimes you don't say things you mean to say.

BLANCH   Meyer.

MEYER   Always listening.

BLANCHE   I'm glad you took me.

MEYER   Likewise.
> (*They continue to dance*)

MEYER   You know, Blanche, when I think—

BLANCHE   I know, of all the girls you could have been stuck
with.

BOTH
Have I told you lately
How much yours truly loves you?
> (*The music stops. They kiss.* TEDDY *enters angrily*)

62

I CAN GET IT FOR YOU WHOLESALE

MEYER (*Anxiously*) Teddy—

TEDDY (*Short*) Meyer, I already told you—

BLANCHE (*Runs after* TEDDY *and stops him*) Oh, Mr. Asch, am I jealous of you! Men are so lucky. They leave the house in the morning. They go to an office. They order people around. They make deals. What does a woman do? She gets the children off to school. She makes the beds. She vacuums the rugs. Four o'clock this afternoon—women all over New York, they'll be cooking. But you—you and Meyer and Harry—you three—you'll be busting with excitement. Will we be a success, a failure? You'll be worrying, sure. But you'll be together. Friends, partners, you'll be alive.

TEDDY (*Pause, then quietly*) The trouble with housework, you can't make a killing at it.

HARRY (*Sober*) Yeah, but will we?

TEDDY (*Holds up crossed fingers*) We just gotta.
(HARRY *puts arms across shoulders of* TEDDY *and* MEYER. *Men exit and* MISS MARMELSTEIN *enters*)

MISS MARMELSTEIN (*To the heavens*) Oh, God, what a business!

BLANCHE Miss Marmelstein, can I help?

MISS MARMELSTEIN You mean it?

RUTHIE (*Entering*) Me, too?

MISS MARMELSTEIN   All right, now, pay attention. Every buyer
—when they sit down in the showroom—if you see they each
get a pad and a pencil you'll be adding eight years to my
life.

BLANCHE   Each buyer—one pad—

RUTHIE   And one pencil.

MISS MARMELSTEIN   All we need is they should please God
start writing the orders—and a point should break!

BLANCHE   Let's give them two pencils.

MISS MARMELSTEIN   Oooh, did that Mr. Bushkin get a bargain
in you!

RUTHIE   Maybe if we rave about the dresses, they'll write up
a couple of orders.

MISS MARMELSTEIN   Even when they write it doesn't count—
until they go into Mr. Asch's office to give him what they've
written. Those buyers—especially that Miss Springer of the
Bon Ton Shops—her I'll take care of myself. Twelve stores
she buys for, and when she starts writing the orders, that's
when you know you're in.

BLANCHE   What a business!

MISS MARMELSTEIN   In less than an hour we'll know if we *have*
a business!

Scene Ten

The orchestra begins the "Ballad of the Garment Trade."
During this number, the showroom is assembled and dec-
orated before our eyes, and the fashion show takes place.

MISS MARMELSTEIN
    If you don't want to get nervous,
    Do yourself a great big service,
    Stay away please far from Seventh Avenue.
    You can lose your sense and reason
    Guessing what style for next season.
    Yes, the dress business
    Will make a wreck of you.

MISS MARMELSTEIN, RUTHIE and BLANCHE
    It's a battle fierce and grim
    That depends on a lady's whim.
    What will Miss and Mrs. America's answer be?

    Will she say with tossing head,
    "In that rag I wouldn't drop dead!"
    Or will she sigh, "Yes, this dress is really me!"

    On guessing what a dame will say,
    A sheer impossibility,
    These poor kids bravely work away,
    And try to build an industry.

I CAN GET IT FOR YOU WHOLESALE

How crazy, bold and reckless
Can human beings be?

ENTIRE COMPANY

Hip, hip, hooray!
For the garment trade.
Give a cheer, the poor shlemiels,
They're heroes every one.

Day after day,
They go undismayed
To the cockamamy job that must be done.

Off to the fray
On their brave crusade,
Gallant Ladies' garment trade!

Go in health, God speed,
Indigestion's breed,
Men and ulcers on parade!

MEYER, HARRY and TEDDY

What a business, what a sap game.
It's about as much a business as a crap game.
Snap or zipper, bow or button,
All we know is all the experts know from nuttin!
So the last line you got by with,
Coming right up is another you could die with.
If you're right, the dough could flow in.
If you're not, you haven't got a pot to sew in!

ENTIRE COMPANY

Off to the fray

On their brave crusade
Gallant ladies' garment trade!

Go in health, God speed,
Indigestion's breed,
Men and ulcers on parade!
(*The music continues as the showroom is assembled and
the buyers enter. Then* TEDDY *starts to narrate the fashion
show. The models enter, show their dresses to the buyers,
and exit*)

TEDDY Number one-four-o, one hundred forty—it's Manette
in a shimmering coat of jewels and a gown that will make
them dream whether they see it or whether they wear it.
Remember your customers, they'll love this combination, so
put down number one forty. (*Second model enters*) Five
eleven. Five-one-one. They talk about spectator sportswear,
you've heard them, you've sold them, or tried to. Well, here's
a one-piece culotte you won't have to sell. Just let the word
get around you're stocking Acme's number five eleven.
(*Third model enters*) Number five-nine-seven. For years
we've all been asking for a number that's got allure and
class. Well, here it is. So pick up your Acme pencils and
start writing your orders on those pads. Five-nine-seven.
(*Fourth model enters*) Five twenty-two. Play suit, right?
Hah! Okay, now watch. See? How about that? Two for
the price of one. There isn't a woman in the country who
won't flip over this one. And the smart buyer will beat her
to it. So, flip, and write, and remember. Five twenty-two.
Five-two-two. Next! (*Fifth model enters*) Nine-o-three. All
right, now, look. Basics come and basics go. Right? But here
is a basic that's not gonna go. Because it's basically sensa-

tional. Girls and boys, here it is. At forty-nine ninety-five, this is the biggest bargain on Seventh Avenue. Make a note of it, kids. Nine-o-three. Acme Modes, nine hundred three. (*Sixth model enters*) One-zero-four. First notice the pinched waist, the daringly simple cut, and the flattering big peplum. Oh, you have noticed. Well, I'm glad you have, because if you hadn't that girl would be working in the Automat tomorrow. Seriously, put down number one hundred and four. (*Seventh model enters*) Number seven-three-four. One of our real elegant creations which you will see in full color in the next issue of—well, I promised *Vogue* I wouldn't tell. Number seven-three-four. (*Eighth model enters*) Number eight-o-o. This is gonna be a hot seller. You have my personal guarantee. It's an Acme teaser. You can wear it for tea—if you have tea in the bedroom. (*Three models stand together*) And now. Our proudest moment. The number that represents for us the meeting of the world's two great streets—Broadway and Seventh Avenue. Here she is—direct from the Great White Way—in Acme's number seven-seven-seven. Miss Martha Mills, wearing Martha Pink.

> (MARTHA MILLS *enters and moves to center.* MISS SPRINGER *rises as the buyers applaud the show.* TEDDY *escorts* MISS SPRINGER *into his office. The other buyers follow. Everybody waits tensely.* TEDDY *returns with a sheaf of orders in his hand*)

TEDDY (*Too quietly*) We're in.

HARRY What?

> (TEDDY *thrusts out the orders.* HARRY *takes them, scans them swiftly*)

68

HARRY   (*Shouts*) We're in! We're in!
(With a gesture of triumph, he scatters the orders like confetti. PULVERMACHER *approaches* HARRY *and shakes his hand.* MRS. BOGEN *comes forward to embrace her son.* BLANCHE BUSHKIN *comes forward to kiss* MEYER. RUTHIE RIVKIN *comes forward and hugs* HARRY. *Then* THEY *all fade into the crowd, leaving* HARRY *alone as* MARTHA MILLS *comes up to him.* HARRY *pulls a jeweler's box from his pocket, snaps it open, revealing a diamond bracelet.* HARRY *dangles the bracelet in front of* MARTHA. *She reaches for it*)

MARTHA   Wow, where'd you get the money to buy that?

HARRY   Never mind. I got it, do you want it?
(HARRY *pulls bracelet back. Holds out his other hand.* MARTHA *smiles wisely, opens her purse, and pulls out a key*)

MARTHA   (*Handing the key to* HARRY) In case I'm a little late getting home from the theatre, here's the key—go right in—and lie down.
(They exchange a look. HARRY *grins.* MARTHA *grins and exits.* HARRY *tosses the key in the air and catches it*)

HARRY   (*Into the mirror, with boyish enthusiasm*) Hello there, Mr. Bogen! Two years ago you were just another poor slob from the Bronx! Today you're the hottest thing on Seventh Avenue. And tonight you're gonna sleep with an actress!
(The music rises in the last triumphant strains of "Ballad of the Garment Trade")

Curtain

69

ACT TWO

Scene One

The terrace of HARRY BOGEN's *brand new, expensively furnished penthouse. All the principals (except* MARTHA MILLS) *have gathered to celebrate the* bar mitzvah *of* BLANCHE *and* MEYER BUSHKIN's *son* SHELDON.

At rise, SHELDON *is finishing what obviously was quite a speech. The orchestra plays under his words.*

SHELDON

> Or walk with kings—nor lose the common touch.
> If neither foes nor loving friends can hurt you
> If all men count with you
> But none too much.
> If you can fill the unforgiving minute
> With sixty seconds' worth of distance run,
> Yours in the Earth and everything that's in it,
> And—which is more—you'll be a Man, my son!"
> (*Pause*)

Thus said the poet Rudyard Kipling. Today I am on the threshold of being a man, thanks to my honored and beloved parents, Meyer S. and Blanche H. Bushkin. I hereby promise I will try my best to be a credit to my country, my flag, my Jewish heritage, my parents, and all their loving friends here assembled, especially Mr. Harry Bogen, who has honored me with this bar mitzvah party in his brand new penthouse terrace apartment. Omain, and I thank you.

> (*When* SHELDON *finishes, there is applause and then* HARRY *comes forward*)

73

HARRY No, no, no, it's the other way around, Sheldon. I'm the one wants to thank you because there's nothing nicer for a man—he's just moved into a new home—(*Gestures to take in the apartment*) the first thing that happens in it should be an occasion like this. (*Puts his arm around Sheldon*) The son of my partner—and friend. (*Applause as* HARRY *pulls a check from his pocket*) Here, Sheldon. A little present—your first year's tuition at college. This is in addition to the fountain pen.

SHELDON (*His eyes pop as he stares at check*) Holy Smoke!

HARRY Yes, Sheldon, holy smoke. But there are presents better than money—if only on this bar mitzvah day we could give them to you.
  (HARRY *sings* "A Gift Today")
  These gifts are just a token
  Of bigger ones unspoken
   From every loving relative and friend.

  Gifts we wish you very much,
  Things you cannot wear or touch,
  Or tell time with,
  Or write with,
  Or spend.

ALL THE MEN
  If we could have the power
  To raise a wand on high,
  Command for you a gift today,

  Wealth we wouldn't wish you,
  Or things that gold can buy.

I CAN GET IT FOR YOU WHOLESALE

What money makes
Money takes away.

ALL

We'd command you
Something special,
Grand and worthy of this day.

MRS. BOGEN

The gift that I would grant you
Is may you never trade
For glory or success or fame
Your own good name,
Yes, your own good name!

ALL

We'd command you
Something special,
Grand and worthy of this day.

MEYER BUSHKIN

The gift that I would grant you
Is when you need a friend,
You'll fine one half as good and true
(*Gesturing toward* HARRY)
As you know who!

ALL

As we all know who!
We'd command you
Something special,
Grand and worthy of this day.

RUTHIE

> The gift that I would grant you
> Is when you meet the one,
> The one you'll love your whole life through,
> She'll love you too,
> Like she's loved by you.

ALL

> If we could have the power
> To raise a wand on high,
> Command for you a gift today,
> Wealth we wouldn't wish you
> Or things that gold can buy.
> What money makes
> Money takes away.
> (SHELDON *dances with his mother*)
> Happy birthday!
> Thirteenth birthday!
> From the ones that love you so.

HARRY

> Good-bye to childish things now,
> To boyish thoughts and ways.
> May love bless every day you know.
> To a boy, farewell,
> To a man, hello!

ALL

> To a man, hello!

MEYER   (*Coming forward*) Now let's get to that food!

BLANCHE   Wait till you taste Mrs. Bogen's blintzes.

76

MRS. BOGEN (*Correcting her*) Ruthie did all the cooking.

RUTHIE (*Modest*) All I did was measure out the flour.

BLANCHE (*Arch, as she herds everybody toward the dining room*) A girl starts with measuring out flour, and, next thing, she's brushing off rice!

MEYER (*Noting* RUTHIE's *embarrassment*) Blanche, for God's sake!

BLANCHE What did I say?

MEYER (*Low*) Don't say nothing! A year already Harry is going with that girl, but from something serious—not a word. Come everybody, eat.
(RUTHIE *and* MRS. BOGEN, *both looking troubled, take over the process of herding the guests toward the dining room. As* HARRY *is about to follow,* TEDDY ASCH *calls*)

TEDDY Oh, Meyer, can I see you a minute.

MEYER Teddy—the food.

TEDDY You, too, Harry.
(*He pulls* MEYER *and* HARRY *back. The three are alone on stage*)

HARRY What about?
(TEDDY *holds up the check* HARRY *just gave to* SHELDON)

TEDDY (*Reads from the check*) "Seven hundred and fifty dollars" (*Turns the check over*) "Bar mitzvah present for Sheldon Bushkin." Drawn on the bank account of Acme

77

Modes, Inc. He can give nice big presents when other people are paying for it.

HARRY (*Flustered*) That dopey Miss Marmelstein. The day she gets something right, they'll give the kids a half day off from school. (*Takes the check and tears it up*) I'll have her draw another check in the morning. On my personal account. Me for the food, kids.
(HARRY *starts to exit*)

TEDDY Meyer, eight months ago there was another check drawn on our account for a diamond bracelet.

MEYER But he tore up that check, too.

HARRY (*Turning back*) Another mistake. What do you want me to do, fire Miss Marmelstein?

MEYER Shhh.

TEDDY No.

HARRY Then what?

TEDDY Forget it.

MEYER Of course forget it. Come on, let's eat.

HARRY Yeah, I'm practically at the table.
(*Exits*)

78

TEDDY   Meyer, the bracelet was for that actress.

MEYER   But he tore up the check. Right in front of us. You saw

TEDDY   Yeah, but did we see him write it again?

MEYER   Teddy, what are you saying?

TEDDY   I'm not saying anything, yet. I'm just thinking.

MEYER   Thinking what?

TEDDY   That you and I, we're maybe getting rooked.

MEYER   Teddy, please. I don't want to hear things like that. Teddy, we're partners. We're friends. We must trust each other.

TEDDY   You do the trusting. I'm gonna do some looking.
(MANETTE, *slightly tipsy, comes out of dining room*)

MANETTE   Oh, Mr. Asch, I'm keeping a place warm for you.
(*She giggles.* MEYER *laughs*)

MEYER   (*Sings*)
    We'd command you
    Something special,
    Grand and worthy of this day.
(TEDDY *laughs.* BLANCHE *has entered. She and* MEYER *watch as* MANETTE *and* TEDDY *dance and exit. Then* MEYER *dances with his wife.* SHELDON *enters and cuts in.* MEYER

cuts in on his son and BLANCHE. SHELDON *again interrupts.
He faces his father, rising on his toes to indicate he is
tall enough now to be considered a man.* MEYER *laughs
and exits with his arms around his son and his wife*)

Blackout

Scene Two

Voices are heard in the darkness, from a squawk box.

TEDDY'S VOICE   Miss Marmelstein! The canceled checks for last January. Bring them to my office right away.

ANOTHER VOICE   Miss Marmelstein! Where's that Fisher Fabrics order?

TEDDY'S VOICE   Miss Marmelstein! The canceled checks for February and March. Right away!

GAIL'S VOICE   Miss Marmelstein! Does he want to see eight-o-seven in beige?

TEDDY'S VOICE   Miss Marmelstein! I want the paid bill file for the last six months.

GAIL'S VOICE   Miss Marmelstein! What happened to the shoulder straps on eight-o-seven?
   (*The lights come up on the rear area of the Acme Modes loft*)

BUGGO   (*Pushing a rack of dresses across stage*) Miss Marmelstein!

MISS MARMELSTEIN   (*Harassed*) I'm getting them!

BOY (*Pushing a handcart full of boxes in opposite direction*)
Miss Marmelstein!

MISS MARMELSTEIN (*Frantic*) A minute!

MANETTE (*Runs across clutching her shoulder straps*) Miss
Marmelstein!

MISS MARMELSTEIN (*At end of her tether*) I ordered it!
(*The music starts*)

TEDDY What happened to those bills? I want the paid bills
for the last six months, Miss Marmelstein. I want to know
what's in those books. I want to see every canceled check
in our files.
(*He exits.* MISS MARMELSTEIN, *alone on stage, collapses
into a chair and sings* "Miss Marmelstein")

MISS MARMELSTEIN	OFFSTAGE VOICES
Why is it always Miss Marmelstein?	Miss Marmelstein!
Miss Marmelstein?	Miss Marmelstein!
Miss Marmelstein?	Miss Marmelstein!

Other girls get called by their first names
    right away.
They get cosy, intimay—you know what
    I mean?

Nobody calls me hey, Baby Doll,	Miss Marmelstein!
Or Honey Dear,	Miss Marmelstein!
Or Sweetie Pie.	Miss Marmelstein!
Even my first name would be prefurable,	

82

Barbra Streisand as MISS MARMELSTEIN

I CAN GET IT FOR YOU WHOLESALE

MISS MARMELSTEIN   OFFSTAGE VOICES

Though it's turable,
It might be better—it's Yetta!

Or perhaps my second name—that's Tes-
sye,
Spelled T-e-s-s-y—*e*!

But, no, no, it's always Miss Marmelstein.   Miss Marmelstein!
You'd think at least Miss "M"
They could try.
Miss Marmelstein!   Miss Marmelstein!
Miss Marmelstein!   Miss Marmelstein!
                                Miss Marmelstein!

Oh, I could die!

I'm a very
Willing secretary.
Enjoy my work
As my employer will corroborate.

Except for one disappointment,
One fly in the ointment,
It's great, I mean, simply great!

But the aggravation
Of my situation—
I might as well get it off my chest—
Is the drab appellation,
(Pardon the big words I apply
But I was an English major at CCNY)
The drab appellation
With which I am persistently addressed—

I CAN GET IT FOR YOU WHOLESALE

MISS MARMELSTEIN	OFFSTAGE VOICES
Persistently, perpetually,	
Continually, inevitably addressed!	
(Believe me, it could drive a person posi-	
tively psychosomatic!)	
Why is it always Miss Marmelstein?	Miss Marmelstein!
Miss Marmelstein?	Miss Marmelstein!
Miss Marmelstein?	Miss Marmelstein!
Other girls get called by their nicknames	
right away,	
Slightly naughty or risqué. You know	
what I mean.	
Nobody calls me hey, Coochy-coo,	Miss Marmelstein!
Or Boobaleh,	Miss Marmelstein!
Or Passion Pie.	Miss Marmelstein!
Even "Hey there, Babe," though not re-	
spectable,	
Ain't so objectable.	
It's kind of crummy,	
But chummy.	
'Course if I got married, that would do it.	
So where's the lucky guy! (Huh!)	
Till then it still is Miss Marmelstein.	Miss Marmelstein!
Every day I get more and more fussed.	
Miss Marmelstein	Miss Marmelstein!
Miss Marmelstein	Miss Marmelstein!
Ooh, I could bust!	Miss Marmelstein!

(*As the music stops the switchboard buzzes.* MISS MAR-
MELSTEIN *plugs in*)

84

MISS MARMELSTEIN (*Into phone*) Acme Modes, good morning. Hold it a moment. I'll check. (MEYER BUSHKIN *enters, carrying a dress across his arm*) Mr. Bushkin, you seen Mr. Bogen?

MEYER (*Holds up a dress*) Nice?

MISS MARMELSTEIN (*To* MEYER BUSHKIN) It's adorable.
(HARRY *enters*)

HARRY Lift the double pleats to meet the waistline and it'll go.
(*He picks up* MISS MARMELSTEIN *and swings her around*)

MISS MARMELSTEIN (*Squealing with delight*) Oh, Mr. Bogen!
(*She collects herself and points to switchboard*) Fisher Fabrics are on the phone.

TEDDY (*Entering*) Tell Fisher Fabrics I'll call back.

HARRY *You'll* call back?

TEDDY (*To* MISS MARMELSTEIN) Out. (TEDDY *pulls two checks from his pocket. He thrusts one at* MEYER *and reads aloud*) "Seven hundred and fifty dollars. Bar mitzvah present . . ."

HARRY Miss Marmelstein. Take all the calls inside.
(*She exits*)

TEDDY "Bar mitzvah present for Sheldon Bushkin." Drawn a second time—on the bank account of Acme Modes, Inc.

HARRY My own account was low. It's just a loan. I'll put it back.

MEYER (*Reads from check*) Martha Mills. Two thousand four hundred dollars. Drawn a second time.

HARRY That diamond bracelet. She helped us put over our first line.

MEYER (*Getting more checks from* TEDDY) Martha Mills, three hundred dollars. Martha Mills, three hundred dollars. Three hundred dollars a week she gets?

HARRY She earns it.

TEDDY Doing what and for who?

HARRY What difference does that make? We're all partners, aren't we?

TEDDY (*Angrily knocks down a pile of dress boxes*) You're a hungry punk going wild in a bakery. This is a dress business we got. Not Aladdin's lamp. Using firm money for your broad! And God knows what else.

HARRY What the hell you got to beef about? You're a partner in your own firm—drawing down three times as much as you ever earned in your whole life—not counting profits.

TEDDY I wanna make sure there's gonna be some profits to count. If I gotta be robbed, I like it done by a guy shoving a gun in my gut. Not by a partner posing as Santa Claus.

HARRY Any time you don't like the way things are going, you know what you can do.

TEDDY   I'm doing it—beginning tomorrow.

MEYER   (*Bewildered*) Doing what?

TEDDY   Beginning tomorrow, *I* sign the checks.

HARRY   (*Exploding*) I'm not *waiting* till tomorrow. I want my apology now!

MEYER   (*Conciliatory*) Harry, don't get so excited. Teddy didn't mean anything.

HARRY   Let him say so.

TEDDY   All I meant—

HARRY   Meyer and I heard what you meant.

TEDDY   I didn't say nothing about Meyer.

HARRY   You said it about Meyer's partner.

MEYER   Why do we have to say anything about anybody?

HARRY   Because one partner on this team doesn't trust the other two.

TEDDY   It's *you* I don't trust. Not Meyer. I'm gonna see that this firm goes back on a solid basis. By making a few necessary changes.

HARRY   This firm is solid enough for me and Meyer. If it isn't solid enough for you—a few changes won't be necessary. Just one will do the trick.

MEYER (*Troubled*) Harry—

HARRY (*Nodding toward* TEDDY) Meyer, he started this. Let him finish it.
> (TEDDY *hesitates, clearly uncomfortable about the fact that* HARRY *has forced him into a corner. He looks from* MEYER *to* HARRY, *as* HARRY *puts his arm around* MEYER, *separating him from* TEDDY)

TEDDY But Meyer . . . (*He erupts angrily*) Okay. I'll have my lawyer talk to yours in the morning.
> (*He slams out*)

MEYER (*Dazed*) Harry, what does it mean?

HARRY (*Smooth*) It means we don't need him any more, and he knows it. It means that list of buyers he came in with, they're mine now, ours.

MEYER (*Worried*) Harry, you're sure it's all right?

HARRY (*Confident*) All right? Meyer, it's what I've been working for. From now on, Meyer, we're gonna split the take just two ways—you and me. We are gonna go down to the bank this afternoon. We'll open a nice little special account in the name of Meyer S. Bushkin.

MEYER Why?

HARRY Now that Teddy's out of the way, we're in the clear. Just you and me. We'll get rich. The way everybody else

88

does it. We'll draw money out of the business and put it in your special bank account.

MEYER I don't understand why, Harry.

HARRY We write checks on that account—made out to cash—whenever we need money. Blanche wants a fur coat? Draw out the cash.

MEYER Wow!

HARRY Sheldon's college tuition? Draw out the cash. You see, Meyer, with the tax situation, it's the only way a business man can skim off the gravy. It's perfectly legitimate. You don't have to worry about a thing. I'll take care of everything. Meyer, they're playing our song.
       (*He walks* MEYER *off, then turns back and, alone on stage, goes into his dance of triumph*)

HARRY
    Money!
    If you want it, go out and get it—if you got it, you got
        everything!
    Blanche wants a fur coat,
    Blanche gets a fur coat.
    Martha wants a diamond bracelet,
    Martha gets *two* diamond bracelets.
    Harry wants money,
    Meyer writes out a check made out
    To cash.
    I got it made!
Harry Bogen. Harry Bogen . . . A hungry young punk going wild in a bakery . . . Well, Vanderbilt went wild.

Morgan went wild. Astor went wild. And those boys are heroes! Did you ever hear of a Seventh Avenue Robber Baron? Well, meet Harry Bogen the First!

(*He swaggers off as the music mounts to a climax*)

Blackout

SCENE THREE

Acme Modes, Inc. The rear area of the loft. MISS MARMEL-STEIN *is wandering about.*

MISS MARMELSTEIN (*calls*) Mr. Bogen . . . Mr. Bushkin . . . Somebody! (MANETTE *comes across*) All right, Manette, you seen Mr. Bogen?

MANETTE Drop dead.

MISS MARMELSTEIN What's with you?

MANETTE Can't a person feel lousy?
(*She exits*)

MISS MARMELSTEIN (*Shouts after her*) What about *this* per-son? (MEYER BUSHKIN *enters, carrying a dress*) Oh, Mr. Bushkin, Fisher Fabrics have been calling all morning.

MEYER What do they want?

MISS MARMELSTEIN They say we're late with our payments.
(MEYER *stops and turns*)

MEYER (*Incredulous*) Late with our payments? Us?
(HARRY *enters*)

HARRY Relax. These dopey piece-goods houses. I spoke with
Mr. McKee of Fisher Fabrics just yesterday—I've taken
care of everything. (*To* MISS MARMELSTEIN) That case of
Scotch go up to McKee's apartment?

MISS MARMELSTEIN Yesterday afternoon.

HARRY The three dresses for his wife?

MISS MARMELSTEIN Buggo took them over.

HARRY Good. Then you can forget about that call. Just get
me those sales figures I asked for. (*Glances at his wrist
watch*) I got a date at the bank in twenty minutes.
(*She exits*)

MEYER Harry, why are you going to the bank?

HARRY Don't worry, Meyer, it's not to borrow. I'm just going
to let them carry us for a week or two, until our accounts
receivable start rolling in.

MEYER What put us where we have to be carried? Buying
out Teddy Asch, maybe?

HARRY Nah, you never get behind by unloading a freeloader.

MEYER Harry, did we expand too much?

HARRY   Say, that's a hot number. Why don't you make it in green and blue and orange, too, and, Meyer, will you make . .
  (RUTHIE *enters*)

MEYER   Ruthie. It's a pleasure to see you. And such a nice dress.

RUTHIE   It's Acme.

MEYER   Ten-o-two.
  (*He gives* HARRY *a quick, uneasy glance, then exits*)

RUTHIE   (*Crisp*) Harry, did you send a case of whiskey to the credit manager of Fisher Fabrics?

HARRY   (*Sings to* RUTHIE)
               Have I told you lately
               You look so lovely?

RUTHIE   And three dresses to his wife?

HARRY   (*Nods, still singing*)
               Each time I see you

RUTHIE   Harry Bogen, how could you be so stupid?

HARRY   (*Still singing*)
               My heart melts away.

RUTHIE   Anybody knows the minute you try to bribe a credit man, it's all over the trade that you're desperate for cash.

93

HARRY *(Still singing)*
In the rush of little every-day things
(He lifts her up in the air)

RUTHIE *(Annoyed)* Harry, I work in a law office. We have clients. One of them happens to be Fisher *(She slaps him and he sets her down slowly)* Fabrics. Now, you take me seriously. I'm Ruthie Rivkin, your friend. Mr. McKee's calling a meeting of all your creditors: Saltzman Rayons, Feldman Woolens, O'Casey Silks.
(MISS MARMELSTEIN appears with a sheet of paper)

MISS MARMELSTEIN Mr. Bogen, here are those sales figures. *(HARRY snatches the figures, but he continues to look at RUTHIE. MISS MARMELSTEIN glances nervously at her wrist watch)* Your appointment at the bank is in five minutes.
(She exits)

RUTHIE Don't go, Harry. Mr. McKee called your bank from my boss's desk. They won't lend you a penny.

HARRY *(Sullen)* If they don't, somebody else will.

RUTHIE You're not scared?

HARRY If you can't stand heat, stay out of the kitchen.

RUTHIE Then what Murray said was true.

HARRY Who's Murray?

RUTHIE You know I work for him. He said creditors don't call meetings without good reason. He said—

94

HARRY (*Sharply*) I'm a crook?

RUTHIE Harry, is it true?

HARRY You worried?

RUTHIE Yes.

HARRY Nobody has to worry about Harry Bogen.

RUTHIE That's what Murray said. When I asked him if I could come up here.

HARRY (*Angry*) Why did you have to ask Murray?

RUTHIE I can't take time off during a business day without making some sort of explanation.

HARRY The one you made must have been a beaut. Don't look so innocent. Your Murray represents my creditors. Why the hell should he give you time off to come up here and warn me. Unless—unless you and he are pretty chummy?

RUTHIE As a matter of fact, we are. He's asked me to marry him.

HARRY Slobs like McKee. Jerks who run banks. You expect them to walk out on you. (*Furious*) Go ahead, marry him, who's stopping you?

RUTHIE (*Sings* "A Funny Thing Happened")
You don't have to shout.

I CAN GET IT FOR YOU WHOLESALE

From now on I'm out
Of the kitchen!

What's more I can't stand
Your cigarette brand,
And I'm switchin'!
I'm unhappy with things the way they've occurred.
It is time to face facts and not mince a word.
Certain parties named Bogen are getting the bird.
Au revoir, fare thee well, and good-bye!
(*She starts to leave then turns around angrily*)
And I'll tell you why!

A funny thing happened
On my way to love,
I lost the young fella
I'd been dreaming of.
He changed while I waited
And hoped for his call
To someone who's no fun at all.

So I'll start forgetting.
What else can I do?
And much thanks for letting
Me practice on you.
It's farewell, my lovely.
Excuse, please, my dust.
Unravel and travel I must.

No tears, no hurt surprise!
It's with a pleasant glow I realize

If I had that much love,
So deep, true and strong

I CAN GET IT FOR YOU WHOLESALE

All ready to hand you,
My dear Mister Wrong,

Just think of the treasures,
The joy and delight
I'll give to my own Mister Right,
My own
Mister Right!

HARRY

So hasta la vista,
Ta-ta, toodle-oo,
The world will keep turning.

RUTHIE

But not around you.
There's someone else waiting
Who's more than a friend.

HARRY

Best wishes and dishes I'll send.

RUTHIE (*Sarcastic*) Thank you so much.

RUTHIE and HARRY

So long, I'm on my way.
Thanks for the buggy ride, and may I say.

HARRY	RUTHIE
If you had that much love	If I had that much love,
So deep true and strong,	So deep true and strong
How come it's so easy	All ready to hand you,
To tell me so long?	My dear Mister Wrong,

And hurry to Murray.
How quick can you fall?
Oh, no!
It couldn't be so.
What a stall,
You never loved me at all.

Just think of the treasures,
The joy and delight
I'll give
As long as I live
Day and night
To my own Mister Right.

(RUTHIE *snatches her coat and exits*)

Blackout

SCENE FOUR

The Club Rio Rhumba. The bartender, cigarette girl, and waiter are at the bar at the left. They are idly rolling dice. MARTHA MILLS *enters down the steps and trips.*

MARTHA   Oh, you didn't fix that damn step yet.

MARIO   We're going to tomorrow.

MARTHA   Yeah, yeah, I know.

MITZI   Thanks for the tickets, Miss Mills.

EDDIE   We loved you in the new show.

MARIO   Wish you did more.

MARTHA   Well, I don't.
       (TEDDY *comes out*)

TEDDY   Hi, there.

MARTHA   Hi, where. What'll you have—to drink?

TEDDY   Scotch and ginger ale.

MARTHA   You're kidding! (*To* MARIO) The usual. Mr. Asch,

99

you're probably wondering why I asked you to meet me here.

TEDDY No. It's about Harry and I wish it weren't.

MARTHA You're kind of cute. However—

TEDDY Your checks from Acme Modes have begun to bounce.

MARTHA Like tennis balls, and what's more, last night Harry asked me to loan him all the jewels he gave me.

TEDDY Wow! It happened a lot faster than I expected.

MARTHA It's certainly a helluva lot faster than *I* expected. Who's the new dame?

TEDDY He hasn't got one.

MARTHA Come on. You know he's got another—(*Pause*) fashion consultant.

TEDDY No, I swear. Oh, there's his friend from the Bronx.

MARTHA Shirley?

TEDDY Ruthie.

MARTHA What's the difference? Dumped again. Men like Harry Bogen always start with me and end up marrying some little broad who reminds them of their mother.

TEDDY You're on the wrong track, baby—I mean, Miss Mills.

From what I've been hearing on the Avenue—and from what you just told me—I think Harry's busted.

MARTHA   It'll kill him.

TEDDY   Never. He's got more guts than anybody I ever knew. I don't like him, but I admire him.

MARTHA   If Harry's busted, where does that leave you?

TEDDY   Harry had to buy me out, and I don't mind telling you it cost him a bundle.
   (*A pause*)

MARTHA   Mr. Asch, may I ask you a personal question, baby?

TEDDY   That's what I've been waiting for.

MARTHA   You *are* cute! Hi!

TEDDY   (*Sings* "What's In It For Me?")
   High, high, high, baby, on a windy hill
   We'll kiss and sigh, baby, while our hearts stand still.
   Before we try, baby, climbing merrily—
   One minute, what's in it for me?

   (I'm just asking.)

   Deep, deep, deep, baby, like waves on a shore
   Our love will sweep, baby, with a mighty roar.
   Before we leap, baby, hit that chilly sea—
   One minute, what's in it for me?

I CAN GET IT FOR YOU WHOLESALE

You want the faintest idea of who'll pay the bill?

MARTHA   That's right.

TEDDY
>   Well, let's go get our feet wet and climb
>   That windy hill.

MARTHA   I'm not the outdoor type.

TEDDY
>   Far, far, far, baby, up in heaven's blue
>   We'll ride a star, baby, where each wish comes true.
>   Till we depart, dear baby, aeronautically,

MARTHA
>   One minute, what's in it

TEDDY
>   One minute, what's in it

MARTHA
>   One minute, what's in it for you?
>   (*They dance*)

Scene Five

Acme Modes Showroom. The office door is open. MISS MARMELSTEIN *is on the phone.* TOOTSIE MALTZ *enters through swinging doors. He looks around uneasily.*

MISS MARMELSTEIN *(Tense, into the phone)* Acme Modes. I'm sorry, no, Mr. Bogen is not here now. I don't know when he'll be back. No, I don't know where he is. *(Her voice rises angrily)* There *is* no trouble! *Nothing* is wrong! Good-bye!
  (She slams down phone and sees TOOTSIE*)*

TOOTSIE Is Harry around?

MISS MARMELSTEIN *(Suspicious)* What do *you* want?

TOOTSIE I, uh, I heard he was in trouble, so I—

MISS MARMELSTEIN *(Sharp)* You better go see a doctor—get the wax out of your ears! You're hearing cockeyed! (MR. PULVERMACHER *enters. Her manner changes at once. She smiles eagerly)* Oh, hello, Mr. Pulvermacher. What a surprise! Seeing you here, I mean—seeing you here.

PULVERMACHER I've been hearing rumors.

MISS MARMELSTEIN *(All innocence)* Rumors? What type rumors?

(PULVERMACHER *does not answer. Throughout scene he wanders about, peering into the office, out into the factory, into the models' room*)

TOOTSIE (*To* MISS MARMELSTEIN) Could I just see Harry a minute?

PULVERMACHER Sure, take a taxi down the lawyer's office where his creditors are giving him the third degree this minute.
(TEDDY *enters*)

MISS MARMELSTEIN It's not true! I mean, sure, he's down there—but only just answering a few unimportant small little tiny questions.

TEDDY Like where did all the money disappear?

MISS MARMELSTEIN Mr. Asch, you ought to be ashamed of yourself! Spreading malicious rumors about a fellow colleague!

TEDDY My fellow colleague is today getting a taste of what he did to you—(*Nods to* PULVERMACHER) and to you.
(*He nods to* TOOTSIE)

PULVERMACHER How did you escape?

TEDDY I didn't. When he bought me out—like a dope I took notes. (*To* MISS MARMELSTEIN) For this we should feel ashamed?

MISS MARMELSTEIN There's absolutely nothing wrong. Just a small innocent friendly little creditors' meeting.

TEDDY These nice friendly little creditors are going to examine Mr. Bogen's books.

MISS MARMELSTEIN They will not!

TEDDY Oh, yes, they will. I happen to be one of them.

MISS MARMELSTEIN They won't find anything.

TEDDY Five will get you ten they find enough to send my former colleague up the river.

PULVERMACHER How very interesting.
(*He exits*)

MISS MARMELSTEIN (*To* TEDDY) You're just sore because Mr. Bogen bought you out.

TEDDY With what? Paper? There's a rumor you got three thousand dresses on the rack. I'll give you real money for them. Five bucks apiece.
(*He pulls out check book and pen*)

MISS MARMELSTEIN Five bucks apiece—are you crazy or something? Those garments cost us twenty-three forty-five to make!

TEDDY This firm is finished. Five bucks apiece. Grab it while

I'm still in a favor-doing mood. Mr. Bogen will thank you for being so smart!

(*The employees have entered during scene. They stand in the background, listening uneasily*)

MISS MARMELSTEIN   Mr. Bogen doesn't need no favors from nobody! This firm is one hundred percent solid!

TEDDY   You better get *your* ears fixed. Just open a window. You'll hear what they're saying. All up and down the street. If I was you, I'd lock them doors. Any second now, any guy ever shipped Harry Bogen a yard of velvet—a box of buttons—anything ain't been paid for yet—is gonna bust right in here and grab it all back. (*The employees remain silent.* TEDDY *explodes*) Why the hell do you stick with him? The roof's fallen in—and you don't move! (*They stare at him*) That little government man is gonna walk in here and nail up a sign on this door—(*He punches it open*) bankrupt!

(*He exits*)

MISS MARMELSTEIN   They wouldn't dare! Not to Mr. Bogen!

BOY   Here we go again!

MISS MARMELSTEIN   (*Sings* "What Are They Doing To Us Now?")
     As we get older,
     There's nothing surer,
     The rich get richer.
     The poor get poorer.
     Those small misfortunes

I CAN GET IT FOR YOU WHOLESALE

All start to pile up,
And it gets harder
To keep a smile up.

But we keep hoping,
While old dreams linger,
That we'll get lucky one fine day.
Then once again fate
Gives us the finger.
Once again with a sigh,
We look up to the sky,
With a quizzical eye,
And quietly say:

ALL

What are they doing to us now?
What's the latest ruin to us now?
Someone up there is getting careless.
What are they doing to us now, anyhow,
What are they doing to us now?

MISS MARMELSTEIN

Makes no difference if a man is slave or king!
Born he always is to pain and suffering!
Naked, he's pushed out his new life to begin!
Ain't enough, the awkward way he came in.
Wham! Before he understands just why he's here,
Clop! Comes from the Doc a big smack on the rear.
From then on continuous without a stop,
Ow!—life's the same old story—always
Clop! Clop! Clop!

ALL

> Clop! Clop! Clop!
> Clop! Clop! Clop!

MISS MARMELSTEIN

> Science keeps advancing, always on the run.
> All they seem to do is take from life the fun.
> Smoking, oh no no! It wears your heart away.
> Drinking shrinks for you the liver, day by day.
> Eating makes you fat. Your weight you gotta check.
> Sex—you do, you don't—you end a nervous wreck.
> Future generations we had ought to warn.
> Hey! Hey, there, do yourself a favor!
> Don't get born!

ALL

> Don't get born!
> Don't get born!
>
> What are they doing to us now?
> What's the latest ruin to us now?
> Someone up there is getting careless.
> What are they doing to us now, anyhow,
> What are they doing to us now?
>> (*As the number progresses, workmen move in and out, carrying away furnishings. When the number reaches its climax—and the entire showroom has been taken apart—*HARRY *enters and stares in shocked astonishment at the ruins of his firm. An official looking man enters with a large white sign, which he nails on the door. The sign is covered with small print, but one word stands out boldly and clearly: BANKRUPT*)

Blackout

MRS. BOGEN's *kitchen in the Bronx. She is standing at a gas range, staring off into space, a troubled look on her face.* HARRY *enters. He carries a gift-wrapped box. She turns. For a few minutes they stare at each other in searching silence.* HARRY *breaks it*

HARRY   (*Sings cheerfully*)
        Momma momma momma momma
        Why did you have to be
        Made so perfectly, mamamiu?
(*He falters. He speaks quietly*) How did you find out?

MRS. BOGEN   I went to the park—like every day—to get a little sun. Instead—from my friend Ethel—I got *Women's Wear.*

HARRY   (*Bitter*) Some friend.

MRS. BOGEN   Every day we sit on the same bench. Two whole years—right there under her nose—me and my silver fox. To pay me back a little, she's entitled.

HARRY   Ma, listen—

MRS. BOGEN   Don't say another word, no not another word. Sit down, relax, you're safe at home now.
      (*She pushes him gently into a chair at table. She sings* "Eat a Little Something" *as she moves back and forth*

between the stove and the table, setting food before him.
HARRY *sits in silence*)

Eat a little something.
Try a little something.

Things won't look so bad
Once you've had
A bite or two.

Chew a little something.
Touch a little something.

Eat it while it's hot.
So why not?
It's good for you.

Force yourself—
Just a taste!
Go ahead, start in.

Such a home-cooked meal
Who could waste?
It's a sin.

Eat a little something.
Try a little something.

Let the troubles wait.
Clean the plate.
Here, start with these.

Eat a little something.
Please!

MRS. BOGEN
Eat a little something.

Try a little something.
Things won't look so bad
Once you've had
A bite or two.

Chew a little something.
Take a little something.

Eat it while it's hot.
So why not?
It's good for you.

Force yourself
Just a taste
Go ahead, start in.
Such a home-cooked meal

Who could waste?
It's a sin.

HARRY (*Talking as* MRS. BO-GEN *keeps singing*) Ma, listen. Bankruptcy—what you read in *Women's Wear*—it ain't so terrible. Ma, it looks bad—what came out at the hearing this afternoon. But only if you don't know the facts. Sure, there was a special bank account, but it was in Meyer's name. All the money from the firm went into the account. And then it was taken out again. The evidence shows it was Meyer took it out. Don't you see, Ma, I'm clean. Meyer says he gave the money to me. So we could fool the income tax department. But there was no proof, Ma, no proof. Nothing to show where the money went. The referee, the judge, he understood. That's why, downtown in court—he said it's Meyer, not me, Ma. He ordered Meyer to give back the money. Or Meyer goes to jail. I'm clean, Ma. All perfectly legal. They can't touch me. You understand,

Eat a little something.
Try a little something.

Ma, don't you? Nothing to show where the money went. The referee—the judge—he understood. That's why the referee—the judge—downtown in court —that's why he said it's Meyer. Not me, Ma. It's Meyer who has to account for the money. He ordered Meyer to give back the money. Or he goes to jail. I'm clean, Ma. All perfectly legal. They can't touch me. You understand, Ma, don't you? You understand?

Let the troubles wait.
Clean the plate.
Here start with these.

Eat a little something, please!
(*The music continues*)

MRS. BOGEN Sure I understand. The problem is how can we make Blanche understand? You know how stupid some people are. How selfish. (*Sings*)
Eat a little something.
All she thinks about, that Blanche, the only thing in her head is Meyer. All she worries about is tomorrow morning he's going to jail. (*Sings*)
Force yourself, go ahead,
Take a taste, start in.
People who have room in their heads for only little things like that, what chance have they got to get ahead in the world? The way you did, Harry. The way I did through you. (*Sings*)
Eat a little something!
People like Blanche Bushkin, they don't have closets full of

silver foxes. People like Meyer, they don't get marked clean by a judge downtown. But you and me, Harry? We're different. We know what we want. And we know how to get it. (*Sings*)

> Eat a little something!

You'll need your strength. We'll both need it. For the next Meyer who comes along and gets in our way. Who is he, Harry? You got him maybe picked out already? Make it somebody a little bigger than Meyer, yes? This time for my commission I want mink, not silver fox. Harry, eat. It's good. Your mother made it. Just like she made you, she made these. (*Sings*)

> Eat a little something,
> Please!

(*He sits motionless as the song quietly ends*)

Blackout

Scene Seven

When the lights come up, HARRY *is sitting outside the office of* MAURICE PULVERMACHER. *Inside the office,* PULVERMACHER *is behind his desk.* MISS MARMELSTEIN *stands beside him, holding the phone.*

MISS MARMELSTEIN (*Into the phone*) One moment, please. (*Covers the mouthpiece*) Dr. Stern is not in, Mr. Pulvermacher. He's vacationing in Bermuda.

PULVERMACHER Where else? His patient is having a heart attack on Thirty-ninth Street. Naturally the doctor is in Bermuda.

MISS MARMELSTEIN (*Peering at* HARRY) Mr. Pulvermacher, he's still waiting.

PULVERMACHER Tell him he's waiting for a corpse.

MISS MARMELSTEIN What can it hurt to see him?

PULVERMACHER I took you back on condition that you never mention his name!

MISS MARMELSTEIN (*Laughs*) I didn't. (*Into the phone*) One moment, please. (*Covers the mouthpiece*) Mr. Pulvermacher, are you sure it's your heart?

114

PULVERMACHER Shooting pains from here to here. No, it's
my scalp.

MISS MARMELSTEIN (*Into the phone*) It's very urgent. Mr.
Pulvermacher has these pains in his chest.

PULVERMACHER *Very—severe—pains!*
    (HARRY BOGEN *enters*)

MISS MARMELSTEIN (*Into the phone*) These very severe
pains—

HARRY (*To* MISS MARMELSTEIN) You sure got here fast.

MISS MARMELSTEIN A girl's gotta eat.

HARRY Forget the doctor. Send down for a container of hot
tea.

PULVERMACHER What for?

HARRY Tannic acid. It always helped my father.

PULVERMACHER (*To* MISS MARMELSTEIN) Hot tea.

MISS MARMELSTEIN (*On the phone*) We won't be needing
you, Doctor.
    (*She hangs up and exits*)

HARRY Sorry I was out when you dropped in on me the other
day.

PULVERMACHER All right, Harry. What do you want from me
this time?

HARRY   Well, if you can spare it, twenty-two thousand dollars.

PULVERMACHER   Everything changes. Even the way people borrow money. In my day it was always round figures. Today it's twenty-two thousand. Such a curious funny number. It says here in the paper—by tomorrow morning, unless Meyer Bushkin turns over forty-two thousand dollars he goes to jail. Harry. That's all you got away with? Twenty thousand?

HARRY   You know how the money goes. I'm young. I got outside interests.

PULVERMACHER   Yeah, I've seen her. I had a few myself forty years ago—when I had my bankruptcy. So now you want to take your twenty thousand—my twenty-two—and save Meyer's neck, because you're sorry. Or maybe you've seen your mother?

HARRY   Look, this ain't no gypsy tea room. I came here to get my palm greased, not read. You got the money? You can spare it? Fine. I'll pay it back. With interest.

PULVERMACHER   Out of what?

HARRY   How should I know? I haven't thought that far yet.

PULVERMACHER   Ah, ha!

HARRY   On this street I can always get a job.

PULVERMACHER   A job? You? You're not a shipping clerk any more, Harry. Look. Your name in the papers. A forty-two thousand dollar bankruptcy. You're a big man, Harry. You don't belong on a job any more. You belong here. In my chair. (*Gets up and pushes* HARRY *into chair behind desk*) There. That's what you've always wanted, isn't it? How does it feel?

HARRY Look, if you don't want to lend me the money, okay, just say so, but don't—

PULVERMACHER Oh, I'll lend you the money.
    (*A pause*)

HARRY Why? I took away your whole staff. Miss Marmelstein, your designer, your shipping clerks. Why should you put up the money to get me and Meyer off the hook?

PULVERMACHER I'm still in business, and Meyer is still a good designer.

HARRY Then why don't you just go downtown and buy him out?

PULVERMACHER Because I also want Meyer's partner.

HARRY You want me?

PULVERMACHER I'm getting older. I want a smart tough kid with your talent to help me. And while you're helping, I'll be taking half your salary every week to pay back the twenty-two thousand. You'll see, I'll get more out of you than you'll get out of me.
    (BLANCHE *comes in*)

BLANCHE Mr. Pulvermacher—
(*She pauses. She has seen Harry. She goes to him, stares at him for a moment, then slaps his face*)

PULVERMACHER Meyer is not going to jail. (BLANCHE *turns toward him*) It's the truth.

BLANCHE I don't know what to say . . . how to thank you.

PULVERMACHER (*Nods toward* HARRY) He deserves some of the thanks. He's putting in all the money he has.

BLANCHE (*Stares at* HARRY) I can't thank you, Harry. I don't even understand you. (*To* PULVERMACHER) Mr. Pulvermacher, are you sure?

PULVERMACHER Yes.

BLANCHE Can I tell Meyer?

PULVERMACHER You have my word.

BLANCHE Your word I'll take.
(*She exits*)

HARRY She thinks I did it deliberately. But Meyer liked the money.

PULVERMACHER Who doesn't? But Meyer was fine till you came along.

HARRY I didn't mean to do him in.

PULVERMACHER (*Sarcastic*) Oh, you didn't know what you were doing?

HARRY Not all the time. No. It got out of hand—began snow-balling—Mr. Pulvermacher, I tasted money and I loved it. I hated being poor. I hated living in the Bronx.

PULVERMACHER (*He explodes*) I'm sick of that excuse! I was poor, too, and I'm from the Bronx. I got where I am by being damn good. I went bankrupt because I wasn't good enough—but I worked hard and I paid back every cent, and now when I go home at night, I can face my family. "I was poor." Don't you ever hand out that excuse again. You just think the only success is money!

HARRY (*Bitter*) Am I the only one?
(*Enter* MISS MARMELSTEIN *with container of hot tea*)

PULVERMACHER Miss Marmelstein, he'll be in tomorrow morning, nine o'clock. Sharp!

MISS MARMELSTEIN Oh, Mr.—
(*Claps her hand to her mouth*)

PULVERMACHER Now you can say it.

MISS MARMELSTEIN Mr. Bogen!
(*She shakes his hand, then exits*)

PULVERMACHER Good-bye, Harry.

HARRY (*Strokes the chair behind the desk, speaks wistfully*) It's nice.

PULVERMACHER (*Sharp*) Harry, don't get any ideas.

HARRY Who, me? See you tomorrow, Mr. Pulvermacher.
Nine o'clock

PULVERMACHER Sharp!

HARRY Sharp!
   (*He exits. The office set rolls off.* HARRY *is on Seventh
   Avenue. People, carts, dress racks pass back and forth.*
   HARRY *finds himself facing* RUTHIE)

HARRY (*Low*) Meyer is going to be all right.

RUTHIE How's Harry?

HARRY You know Harry. He always lands on his two feet.
How's Murray?

RUTHIE (*A pause*) Murray who?

HARRY (*He reacts*) You could be making a mistake.

RUTHIE That's a chance I'll have to take. With your brains—

HARRY And your character—

RUTHIE And Papa's ten thousand dollars—
   (*He reacts, then smiles*)

HARRY Look, if you're not doing anything, I know where we
can get a great meal.

RUTHIE (*Laughs*) Yeah, your mother always cooks like tomorrow it's going to be illegal.
   (*He takes her hand and they walk off as the orchestra
   takes up the theme of* "Who Knows?")

Curtain